The Best of Danny Proulx's

Storage and Shelving

POPULAR
WOODWORKING
BOOKS
CINCINNATI, OHIO
www.popularwoodworking.com

READ THIS IMPORTANT SAFETY NOTICE

To prevent accidents, keep safety in mind while you work. Use the safety guards installed on power equipment; they are for your protection. When working on power equipment, keep fingers away from saw blades, wear safety goggles to prevent injuries from flying wood chips and sawdust, wear headphones to protect your hearing and consider installing a dust vacuum to reduce the amount of airborne sawdust in your woodshop. Don't wear loose clothing, such as neckties or shirts with loose sleeves, or jewelry, such as rings, necklaces or bracelets, when working on power equipment. Tie back long hair to prevent it from getting caught in your equipment. People who are sensitive to certain chemicals should check the chemical content of any product before using it. The authors and editors who compiled this book have tried to make the contents as accurate and correct as possible. Plans, illustrations, photographs and text have been carefully checked. All instructions, plans and projects should be carefully read, studied and understood before beginning construction. Due to the variability of local conditions, construction materials, skill levels, etc., neither the author nor Popular Woodworking Books assumes any responsibility for any accidents, injuries, damages or other losses incurred as a result of the material presented in this book. Prices listed for supplies and equipment were current at the time of publication and are subject to change. Glass shelving should have all edges polished and must be tempered. Untempered glass shelves may shatter and can cause serious bodily injury. Tempered shelves are very strong and if they break will just crumble, minimizing personal injury.

 Published by Popular Woodworking Books, an imprint of F+W Publications, Inc., 4700 East Galbraith Road, Cincinnati, Ohio, 45236. First edition.

Visit our Web site at www.popularwoodworking.com for information on more resources for woodworkers.

Other fine Popular Woodworking Books are available from your local bookstore or direct from the publisher.

09 08 07 06 05 6 5 4 3 2

Library of Congress Cataloging-in-Publication Data

Proulx, Danny.
The Best of Danny Proulx's storage & shelving.
p. cm.
Includes index.
ISBN 1-55870-731-X (paperback: alk. paper)
ISBN 1-55870-756-5 (hardcover: alk. paper)
1. Cabinetwork. 2. Shelving (Furniture) 3. Storage in the home. I. Title: The Best of Danny Proulx's storage and shelving. II. Title: Storage & shelving. III. Title.
TT197.P75964 2005
684.1'6--dc22 2004055327

ACQUISITIONS EDITOR: Jim Stack
EDITED BY: Amy Hattersley
DESIGNED BY: Brian Roeth
PRODUCTION COORDINATED BY: Robin Richie and Jennifer Wagner
PHOTOGRAPHIC CONSULTANT: Michael Bowie, Lux Photographic Services, Lancaster Rd., Ottawa, Ontario. (613) 247-7199
COMPUTER ILLUSTRATIONS BY: Len Churchill, Lenmark Communications Ltd., Alden Rd., Markham, Ontario. (905) 475-5222
WORKSHOP SITE PROVIDED BY: Rideau Cabinets, Russell, Ontario. (613) 445-3722

fw
F+W PUBLICATIONS, INC.

ABOUT THE AUTHOR

Danny Proulx is the owner of Rideau Cabinets and is a contributing editor for *CabinetMaker* magazine. He also contributes freelance articles for *Canadian Woodworking, Canadian Home Workshop, Popular Woodworking* and other magazines. His earlier books include *Build Your Own Kitchen Cabinets, The Kitchen Cabinetmaker's Building and Business Manual, How to Build Classic Garden Furniture, Smart Shelving and Storage Solutions, Building Modern Cabinetry, Building More Classic Garden Furniture, Building Cabinet Doors and Drawers, Build Your Own Home Office Furniture, Display Cases You Can Build, Building Frameless Kitchen Cabinets, Building Woodshop Workstations, The Pocket Hole Drilling Jig Project Book* and *Danny Proulx's Toolboxes and Workbenches.*

His Web site address is www.cabinetmaking.com, and he can be reached by e-mail at danny@cabinetmaking.com.

ACKNOWLEDGEMENTS

This is another book of projects that I've enjoyed building, but I could never accomplish it alone. The people close to me are, as always, a big part of this book. My wife, Gale, is constantly helpful and supportive, as is my father-in-law and assistant, Jack Chaters.

Michael Bowie of Lux Photography continues to show his amazing photographic talents and is the person I rely on for photographic expertise. He advises and guides me as I shoot photos for each project. Many of the photos in this book are by Michael. His desire to produce the best results and his expert advice contribute greatly to the final product.

Len Churchill of Lenmark Communications is the talented illustrator who has been working with me and producing the amazing project drawings. He is one of the best illustrators in the business and has an impressive understanding of the woodworking projects he's asked to draw.

As always, the Popular Woodworking Books staff continues to be unbelievably supportive. It's a team with great depth and knowledge including editors Jim Stack and Amy Hattersley, designer Brian Roeth, and so many others who are a part of every page in this book.

TECHNICAL SUPPORT

I often turn to a number of companies for advice and supplies. They are always helpful and are a source of valuable information. They are major players in the creation of my books, and I've listed them in the back of this book under the heading of suppliers. I'd appreciate your support of these fine companies.

METRIC CONVERSION CHART

TO CONVERT	TO	MULTIPLY BY
Inches	Centimeters	2.54
Centimeters	Inches	0.4
Feet	Centimeters	30.5
Centimeters	Feet	0.03
Yards	Meters	0.9
Meters	Yards	1.1
Sq. Inches	Sq. Centimeters	6.45
Sq. Centimeters	Sq. Inches	0.16
Sq. Feet	Sq. Meters	0.09
Sq. Meters	Sq. Feet	10.8
Sq. Yards	Sq. Meters	0.8
Sq. Meters	Sq. Yards	1.2
Pounds	Kilograms	0.45
Kilograms	Pounds	2.2
Ounces	Grams	28.4
Grams	Ounces	0.035

table of contents

1

1

2

3

introduction

I enjoy writing practical woodworking books for woodworkers who have full-time jobs like millions of people, but love to get into the woodshop at every opportunity. Once again this book, like most of my others, is dedicated and directed to those special people.

The furniture projects in this book are not intended to be family heirlooms. They are practical, cost-efficient furniture and storage projects for everyday use for a growing family. They are designed to be rugged and should serve their intended purpose for 10 or 15 years. If you're looking for a Queen Anne-style chest or how to hand cut dovetails, many books are available on those and other subjects.

My book writing has always been directed toward the everyday needs of people who want "working" furniture. I've spent years building one-of-a-kind pieces, but I no longer build that type of furniture. I'm more interested in designing a functional piece of furniture for people who, like myself, need a simple bookcase, a child's bed or a nice cabinet for the new TV.

Throughout the book I've written small information pieces under the heading "Shop Talk." They discuss, and illustrate in some cases, ways to make doors and drawers, as well as procedures that I've used in the shop over the years. I hope they are helpful and further enhance your shop time.

The first chapter deals with modern joinery hardware and options, which can be used to build these projects. In chapter two I detail the concepts and construction techniques needed to build base and wall cabinets that can be used in the basement, workshop, laundry room or just about any other room where solid, practical storage cabinets are needed. All you have to do is decide what sheet material to use. You might pick melamine particleboard for low-cost quality cabinets or veneer-covered plywood for a higher-end unit. I've also included instructions on how to build custom countertops and work tops in this chapter.

In chapters three through seven I've tried to address most of the places in your home where furniture is often needed. Chapter three has a number of projects for your children's bedrooms. Projects are directed at children of all ages in this chapter, such as a work center, a bed and a dresser. Building a desk for your teenager might even generate some interest in those homework chores they sometimes try to avoid.

Chapter four addresses a need that many homes seem to have — better storage in the kitchen. We never have enough space for groceries, so the freestanding pantry should be of interest to many of you. In chapter five I deal with basement storage projects, which may be useful to those of us who live in areas with four seasons and just as many clothing changes. Closet organization and improved storage is a popular topic. I've tried to offer a few low-cost solutions for doubling the existing space in most closets.

The family room is the focus in chapter six with an entertainment unit that is easy to make. It can be customized to hold all your television and audio equipment. The last chapter in the book details projects for the master bedroom. You can build them all and you'll have a complete bedroom set or modify one of the projects to match existing furniture.

I hope you enjoy building some of these projects, and that they'll prove as useful in your home as they have in mine. If you have any questions, please send me an e-mail at danny@cabinetmaking.com.

CHAPTER one

Basic Joinery Techniques and Hardware Applications

The last few years have been exciting for those of us in the building materials and hardware industry. Modern plywood, improved particleboard (PB), melamine-coated PB and medium-density fiberboard (MDF) have made a tremendous impact on how we build cabinets.

Some of you have used these composite boards when they were first introduced and may have been disappointed. Today, composite boards have grades with standards, and the products are far superior to the early offerings.

Low-cost sheet material is available. However, it isn't good value for your money and should be avoided. Ask the supplier for cabinet-grade products and pay a little more to get high-quality material. Most often, it's only a few dollars a sheet more, but it's well worth the money. You can make a lot of furniture from one sheet of PB, so a few extra dollars isn't a major issue.

Manufacturers have their own grade systems, but the most common standard is the weight of melamine paper coating and epoxy layers. You'll often see the terms 100 gram or 120 gram, which is the combined weight of the overlay and coating. Cabinet-grade melamine particleboard ranges in coating weights from 100 to 180 grams. The higher grades are usually specified for applications such as medical cabinetry, and the 120-gram board is commonly used for kitchen cabinet construction. A good cabinet-grade board is a low-pressure laminate and not a painted or glue-laid covering.

Joinery Techniques

A groove is a cut made on the long edge, or with the grain, to receive a second panel or piece of wood. It can be cut on a table saw or router table and is used extensively for door and cabinet construction.

Butt joinery is the most basic and commonly used joint. Two pieces of material are joined with glue or glue and hardware, without cutting into either piece.

A tenon is the other half of a groove or mortise joint. It's made using a table saw or router table and can also be cut with hand tools. The simplest method used to cut tenons is with a stacked dado blade on your table saw. However, tenons can just as easily be cut using a regular saw blade and making several passes over the blade.

Dado cuts are similar to grooves, but they typically travel across the grain. They are machined in the same way grooves are cut, using a table saw or router.

Rabbet cuts are simply grooves on the edge or end of a panel or piece of lumber. Again, the table saw is the easiest tool used to form a rabbet, but many woodworkers also use a router that's handheld or in a table. Rabbet joints are often the joint of choice for large panel joinery when building cabinet cases. Glue can be used alone, or with hardware, to secure the joint.

Most other joints in common use are combinations of the previous basic joinery options. For example, the half-lap joint pictured here is formed by attaching two pieces of wood with rabbet joints cut on the ends.

Many of the drawer boxes used in the projects can be joined with box joints. I've detailed both butt and rabbet joinery for box corners, but you may wish to use a more involved joint such as the box joint shown in a "Shop Talk" at the end of this section.

Biscuit joinery is a form of joinery used when a hidden connection between two panels is required. The biscuit jointer cuts an elliptical slot in two pieces of material to be joined then glue is put in the slots and a beechwood biscuit is inserted. The panels are brought together, clamped and left until the glue cures. Water-based glue causes the beechwood biscuits to swell, which further strengthens the joint. It's a great joinery system that all woodworkers should use. Biscuit cutters can be expensive, but you'll find dozens of applications for this tool.

Panel Machinery

Many of the panels used to build the projects in this book will be MDF, melamine-coated PB or veneer-covered plywood. Don't sell these materials short; they are used to build strong and stable furniture, but you must buy high-quality cabinet-grade sheet material. To find cabinet-grade sheet material distributors in your area, visit www.uniboard.com or www.panolam.com on the Internet.

Coated and plain PB and plywood boards are stable materials that are suitable for many cabinet applications. These products are the most common building materials in today's furniture industry. The melamine-coated decorative panels come in a wide range of colors. And best of all, they're already finished. The wood veneer boards can be stained, glued, joined and used like solid wood.

Panel joinery for cabinet case construction often uses the rabbet joint. It's a common corner joint that can be used successfully with glue and clamps or with glue and hardware such as nails or screws. Again, it can be easily and accurately machined on a table saw with a stacked dado blade.

When working with wood, veneer-covered PB or veneer plywood sheets, we have dozens of wood screw hole coverings available. The plug and button are the two common types, but many other styles are available.

Mechanical Joinery

A special PB fastener, called the particleboard screw, until recently has been used only by professional cabinetmakers. It's a great fastener, with superior holding capabilities, but you should be aware of a couple of issues when using this screw.

First, the screw is tapered with a thin shaft and coarse threads. You must drill accurate pilot holes and drive the screw straight into that hole for a positive hold. Poor drilling techniques or improper driving will push the screw through the finished surface or weaken the joint. However, once you become accustomed to using the screw you'll appreciate its fastening power. When you need a strong joint that is able to withstand stress, this is the fastener to use.

Adjustable Shelving

The fixed shelf is gone! Nowadays, everyone wants adjustable shelves in their cabinets. It's a feature that makes sense because it increases the flexibility of any cabinet. Adjustable shelving is easy to install. All that is required are accurately drilled columns of holes and good-quality shelf pins. Quite a few of the projects in this book will feature adjustable shelving.

The simple jig shown here is easy to make. It's nothing more than a piece of plywood with hardwood ends and a thin strip of metal with holes. The drill bit is guided by the holes, and a wood dowel on the bit limits the hole depth.

Hidden Hinges

In the last few years door mounting hardware from Europe has become a popular alternative. The so-called Euro hidden hinge is now widely used as the standard kitchen cabinet door hardware.

Hidden hinges are also classed in terms of degrees of opening. For standard door applications, the 100° to 110° opening hinge is common. But you can purchase hinges that will allow the door to open from 90° to 170°. The term simply refers to the number of degrees of swing that the door can open from its closed position.

The hidden hinge requires a 35mm-diameter hole to be drilled in the door.

These hinges are classified with terms such as full overlay, half overlay and inset. Overlay simply means the distance the door covers the end of the cabinet side panel (sometimes referred to as the gable end).

The hidden hinge comes in two parts: the hinge boss, which is mounted on the door, and the mounting plate, which is attached to the cabinet side or gable end of the cabinet.

The boss is attached to the mounting plate with a screw or a clip pin. The clip-on method is popular because you can remove the door from the mounting plate without disturbing any adjustments.

Assembly Brackets

Attaching countertops during a kitchen project is often accomplished using metal brackets. It's the best method for securing something, like a kitchen countertop, that will have to be replaced in the future.

These brackets come in many shapes and sizes. They provide a quick-connect capability and add strength to any project. They are sometimes used with other joinery hardware to provide extra hold when joint stress is an issue.

Drawer Glides

Modern hardware now gives us the opportunity to vary drawer styles and construction methods. Side- and bottom-mount glides with three-quarter- and full-extension capabilities, along with positive stops and closing features, have opened a world of design opportunities.

Low-cost metal drawer glide sets that consist of two bottom-mount drawer runners and two cabinet tracks are simple to install. This style of new drawer hardware demands special attention to the drawer body width, as most of the glide sets on the market require precise clearances to operate properly. Otherwise, building high-quality drawers is well within the abilities of any woodworker or hobbyist.

High-Pressure Laminates

High-pressure laminates are the best materials for kitchen countertops. But these laminates have many other cabinet applications. I'll use some of these materials for the projects in this book and detail the installation procedures in a chapter two "Shop Talk".

However, you might want to build the safety guide shown here for your table saw and use it when cutting laminates. The guide traps the thin laminate sheet and won't allow it to slip under the saw fence and cause a possible material bind.

Edge Tape

All the colored panels and wood veneers have complementary edge tape that is attached with glue. In some cases, solid-wood edging is installed to protect and accent the beauty of these boards. Most edge tape can be applied with an iron because of the heat-activated glue used on the tape.

Making Solid Wood Panel Glue-Ups

1 Successful wood panel glue ups can be accomplished with your table saw. All that's needed is a well-tuned saw and a little care. First, make certain the table saw blade is sharp, the fence is parallel to the blade, and the blade is at a 90-degree angle to the top surface of your saw.

2 Rip one edge of each board, then reverse, and rip the other edge.

3 Line up the panels making sure they butt tightly together. If there is a gap, rip small amounts off each side until the board is straight. Draw a line across the boards, along each joint line, as an alignment reference. If possible, alternate the growth rings on each board to minimize panel warping and cupping.

4 Apply an even coat of glue to both edges of each panel to be joined. Clamp the boards, alternating the clamps on the top and bottom. Tighten the clamps until the glue begins to squeeze out of the joint. Do not over tighten, as you will starve the joint of glue.

5 Once the glue has set according to the manufacturer's specifications; scrape the joint of hard glue. Sand the panel and cut to the required size.

shop talk | ***Building a Panel Cutting Jig***

1 A panel cutting jig for your table saw will turn crosscutting boards into a simpler and safer task. First, cut a piece of $\frac{3}{4}$" thick sheet material that's approximately 24" wide by 36" long. You'll also need a strip of hardwood that fits snugly, without binding, in one of the miter slots on your table saw. The hardwood strip should be about 30" long so a few inches of the material will extend past the front and rear edges of the sheet material. Most miter slots are $\frac{3}{4}$" wide and about $\frac{1}{4}$" to $\frac{3}{8}$" deep.

Attach the hardwood strip to the bottom face of the panel, parallel to one 24" long edge. Draw a line parallel to the panel's edge to guide the strip placement, being sure to mark it so 1" of panel extends past the blade.

2 Place the panel, with the hardwood strip attached, in the miter slot and cut the panel overhang. This cut will align the panel travel parallel to the saw blade.

3 Use a carpenter's framing square to align a hardwood guide at 90° to the panel's cut edge. Secure the guide with screws.

shop talk | *Installing Doors With Hidden Hinges (the Simple Way)*

Door mounting jigs are available at all woodworking stores. And if you plan to use the hidden hinge for many projects, these jigs are worthwhile. If you use the hidden hinge only occasionally, here's a quick and easy installation method without using a jig.

This method works with all hinge mounting applications. But it's based on using a 95° to 110° standard opening hinge. If you plan to install a nonstandard hinge, such as the 170° model, install the door with a standard hinge boss mounted in the door, then replace the hinge boss with a 170° boss after the door has been hung.

1 First, drill the holes in the door and mount the hinge boss. Then, secure the hinge boss in the hole, making certain it's at 90° to the door edge. Clip the mounting plate on the hinge.

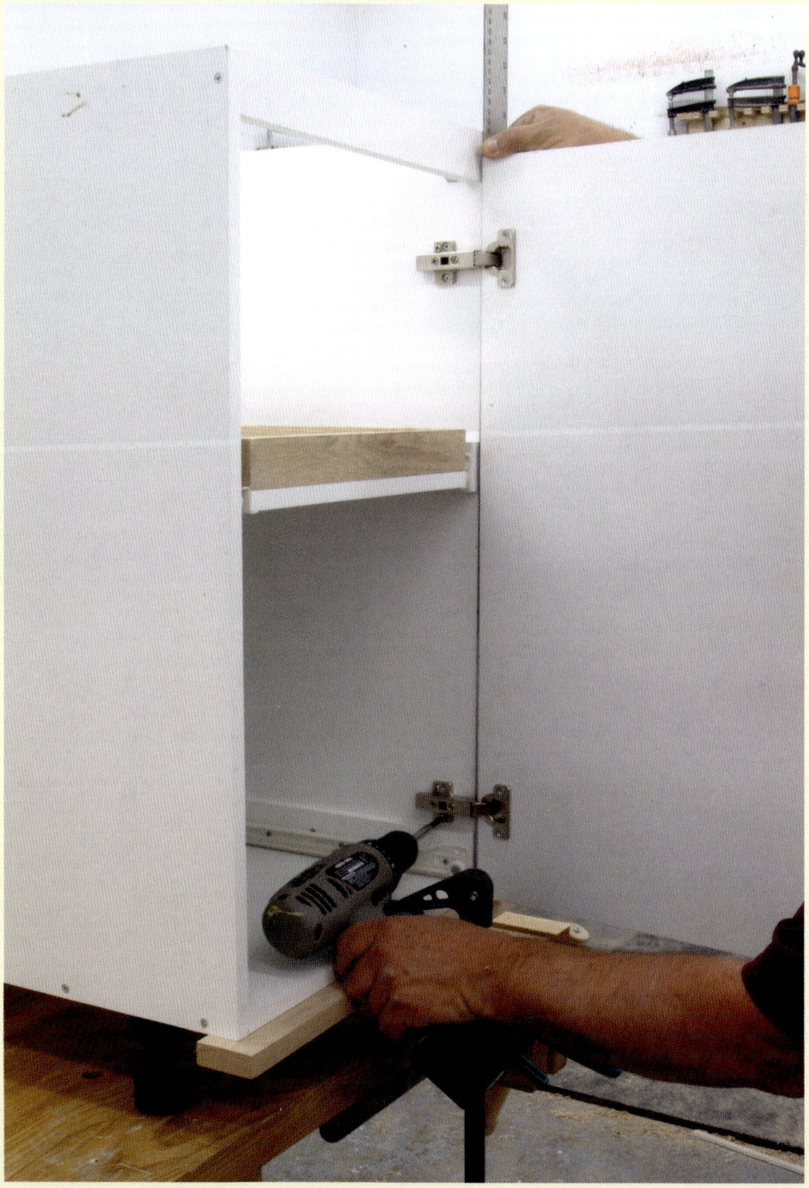

2 Place the door on the cabinet in its 90° open position. A ⅛" thick spacer, between the door edge and the side panel edge, sets the correct door gap. Insert screws through the mounting plate to secure it to the cabinet side.

1 Attach a long 1x2 extension on your table saw miter fence. It will be used to support the finger joint indexing panel.

2 Clamp an indexing panel, which is about 8" high and 24" long, to the extension board on your miter fence. This tall indexing panel will help support large boards as they are pushed through the dado blade. Once secured, cut through the indexing panel. I am setting up and testing this jig with a ½"-wide dado blade.

3 Cut a wood indexing pin, which equals the cut width, and glue it in the notch on the panel.

4 Use a loose indexing pin, which also is the same width as the notch, to set the fixed indexing pin ½" away from the dado blade. Clamp the indexing board securely to the miter fence extension.

5 Cut the two boards to be joined together. The rear board is held tight to the fixed indexing pin, and the front board is set away from the fixed pin, using the loose indexing pin as a guide. Remove the loose indexing pin and make the first cut.

6 The second cut is made with the rear board notch over the indexing pin and the front board tight to the pin. Make the remaining cuts by moving the notches over the pin until all fingers and slots have been formed.

If the test joint is loose, move the indexing panel so the fixed pin is slightly farther away from the blade. If the fingers are too wide for the notches, move the fixed indexing pin toward the blade. Be careful moving the index board because it doesn't take much pin movement toward or away from the blade to dramatically change the finger and slot width.

building custom wood-edged countertops | *page 22*

frameless base cabinets | *page 25*

Storage Cabinets for Every Room

utility wall cabinets | *page 35*

basic bookcase construction | *page 39*

Here are a few cabinets and work tops that can be used in any room. Wood-edged, high-pressure laminate tops can be used for desks, worktables and bathroom, laundry and kitchen cabinets. The upper and lower cabinets can be made with any sheet material to match the room décor. White melamine PB is often used in laundries, kitchens or bathrooms. The wood veneer-covered sheet materials work well as desks or storage cabinets. Plywood sheets are often a popular choice for workshop and garage cabinet bases and uppers.

And who doesn't need another bookcase in the family room or child's room? Here's a simple plan that will help manage all those books and collectibles lying around the house.

PROJECT 1

building custom wood-edged countertops

This countertop style is easily made and well within any woodworker's capabilities. The process involves attaching a solid-wood edge to a panel, called the substrate, and covering the top with high-pressure laminate (HPL).

HPL is made with decorative surface papers, impregnated with melamine resins, which are pressed over kraft paper core sheets. The sheets are then bonded at pressures of 1300 pounds or more per square inch with temperatures approaching 300°F (149°C). The finished sheets are trimmed, and the backs sanded to facilitate bonding. Most manufacturers have over a hundred different patterns available.

High-pressure laminate materials come in two thicknesses. The thinner version is used to manufacture post-formed countertops that are common in almost every kitchen and bathroom. The thicker, general-purpose (GP) laminates are used for applications such as counter tops and work surfaces like desks and tables. The GP material is able to withstand more abuse because of its thickness.

This great-looking wood-edged countertop style has a number of uses. It can be used as a kitchen or bathroom top, as a work center/desk or as a utility countertop. I've used it in dozens of unique projects over the years. And because the laminate is available in 4' × 8' or 5' × 12' sheets, most tops can be made without a seam.

You can use any stable sheet material as the substrate, including particleboard, plywood or medium-density fiberboard. I recommend a minimum ¾"-thick substrate for strength and stability. The wood edge can be any hardwood or softwood that matches or complements the cabinets.

1 Cut the substrate sheet material to the required size. Reduce the desired finished size by $^3/_4$" where the wood edge will be installed. I am using $^3/_4$"-thick particleboard as my substrate for this top.

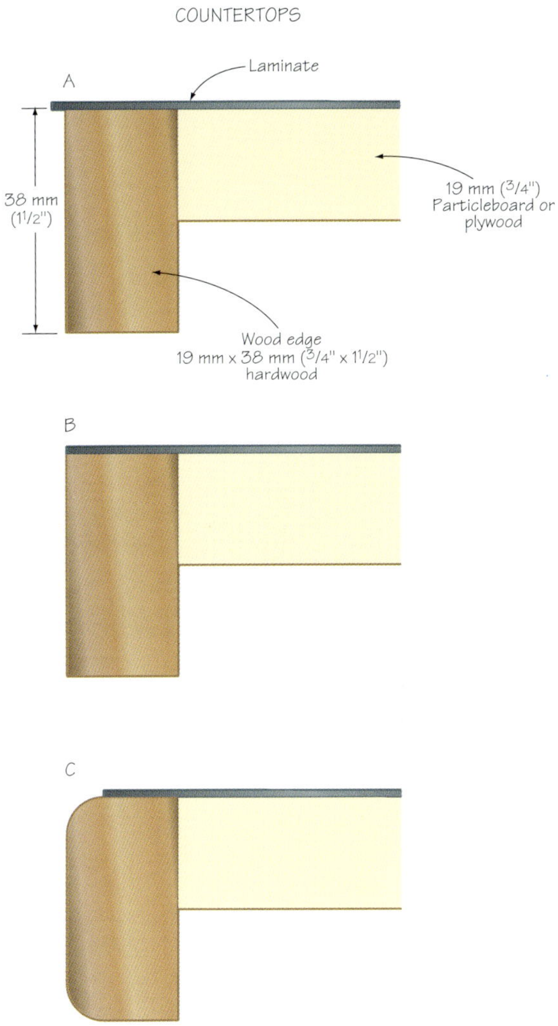

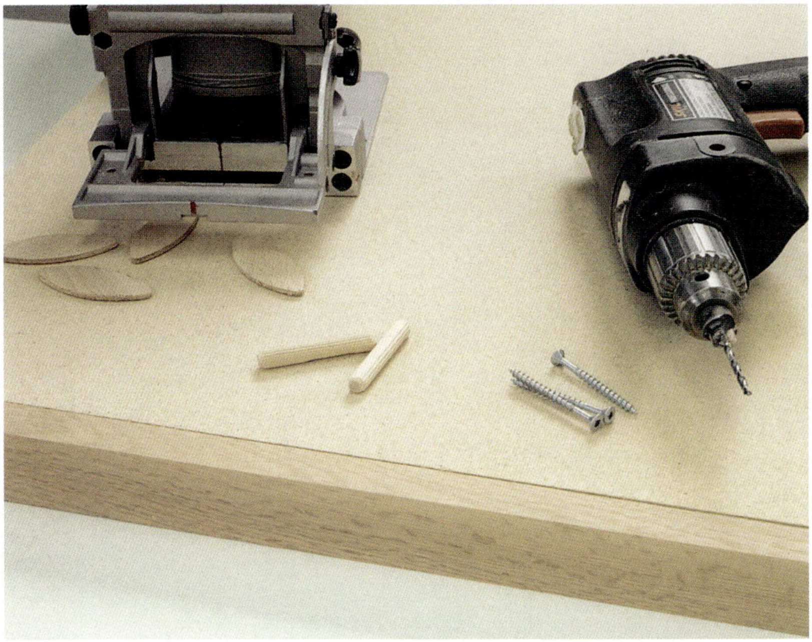

2 Attach the wood edge with glue and screws covered by wood plugs. You can also use dowels or biscuits; any of these three options will work equally well. Be sure the top of the wood edge and the surface of the substrate are perfectly flush. If not, sand both to achieve a flat smooth surface. This is a critical step, as the laminate won't properly bind to an uneven surface.

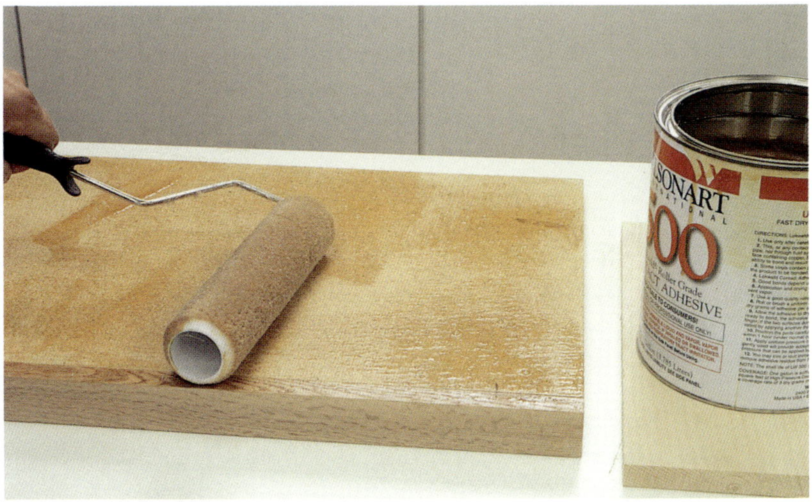

3 Cut the laminate 1" longer than the substrate on all edges. That extra width and length will allow for any slight positioning errors. Apply a contact adhesive to both the underside of the laminate and the top of the substrate. Make certain there's an even coat on both surfaces and all areas are covered. Many types of contact cement are available. I'm using a roller-grade liquid, but brush and spray contact cements are available at most suppliers.

4 The contact cement is set when it's dry to the touch. However, read the instructions listed on your container for best results. This adhesive will bond only to another surface with the same glue applied. Therefore, place dry sticks on the substrate to keep the materials from touching until the laminate is correctly positioned. Be careful — once the two glued surfaces touch, they are bonded! Remove the center stick and press the laminate in place with your hand. Move your hand from the center to the outside edges, pushing out any trapped air bubbles. A pressure roller is the best tool to make certain the laminate is completely bonded to the substrate. If you don't have a commercial roller, use a wooden rolling pin or large wood dowel. Again, roll from the center to the edges, with particular attention paid to the laminate edges.

5 The excess laminate can be cut flush to the wood edge, using a flush-trim router bit. These bits have a guide bearing, which tracks along the substrate and wood edges to cut the laminate flush. Be sure the bit is clean and the bearing is in good shape.

6 A roundover bit in a router is used to make a simple rounded profile on the bottom of the wood edge. The top or laminated surface of the countertop is cut using the same roundover bit. Set the bit so its straight cutters, which are above the curved portion of the bit, cut slightly lower than the thickness of the laminate material. That cutting pass will trim the laminate cleanly and expose the wood under the laminate, as well as rounding over the top edge.

7 The wood edge and laminate profile should look like the end view shown. Once all the cutting has been completed, sand the wood edge smooth and apply a finish.

CONSTRUCTION NOTES

Using general-purpose laminate, which is a thicker material, will provide you with a durable countertop. Stick with the major brands of laminate material for the best results. However, use care when cutting to avoid damaging the laminate. The best router bits are carbide tipped and work exceptionally well for this application. The wood edge in my case was oak, but any species can be used. High-quality material and contact cement will give you perfect results every time.

Some of the adhesives are toxic — particularly the petroleum-based products — so work in a well-vented area. And make sure you closely follow the application directions from the adhesive manufacturer, because it is important to apply them under the appropriate temperature and humidity levels.

PROJECT 2

frameless base cabinets

The basic melamine PB European-style frameless base cabinet is a box with two sides, a bottom board, a top rail and a backboard. There is normally a door or a door-and-drawer combination with fixed or adjustable shelving inside the cabinet. However, all cabinets are not the same width. We often need specific width cabinets to fill dedicated spaces. So, I'll show you how to calculate the door size based on the cabinet width.

Standard utility base cabinets are 36" high when complete. That height includes the cabinet base support and the countertop thickness. For these cabinets, I will be using plastic adjustable legs, but you can construct a wood base just as easily.

The following table lists all the box or case, parts needed to build a frameless base cabinet using $\frac{5}{8}$" melamine PB. However, substitute any sheet material or any thickness you desire. If you use $1\frac{1}{16}$"- or $\frac{3}{4}$"-thick sheet goods, simply make small changes to the $\frac{5}{8}$" cutting list.

cabinet parts list

CABINET WIDTH	TWO SIDES D x H	ONE BOTTOM D x W	ONE BACK W x H
12" (305mm)	23⅜" x 31" (594mm x 787mm)	23⅜" x 10¾" (594mm x 273mm)	12" x 31" (305mm x 787mm)
15" (381mm)	23⅜" x 31" (594mm x 787mm)	23⅜" x 13¾" (594mm x 349mm)	15" x 31" (381mm x 787mm)
18" (457mm)	23⅜" x 31" (594mm x 787mm)	23⅜" x 16¾" (594mm x 426mm)	18" x 31" (457mm x 787mm)
21" (533mm)	23⅜" x 31" (594mm x 787mm)	23⅜" x 19¾" (594mm x 502mm)	21" x 31" (533mm x 787mm)
24" (610mm)	23⅜" x 31" (594mm x 787mm)	23⅜" x 22¾" (594mm x 578mm)	24" x 31" (610mm x 787mm)
27" (686mm)	23⅜" x 31" (594mm x 787mm)	23⅜" x 25¾" (594mm x 654mm)	27" x 31" (686mm x 787mm)
30" (762mm)	23⅜" x 31" (594mm x 787mm)	23⅜" x 28¾" (594mm x 730mm)	30" x 31" (762mm x 787mm)
33" (838mm)	23⅜" x 31" (594mm x 787mm)	23⅜" x 31¾" (594mm x 806mm)	33" x 31" (838mm x 787mm)
36" (914mm)	23⅜" x 31" (594mm x 787mm)	23⅜" x 34¾" (594mm x 883mm)	36" x 31" (914mm x 787mm)

CUSTOM CABINET WIDTHS

You may need a cabinet width that's not on the chart for your specific application. That isn't a problem. If, for example, I required a 31½"-wide base cabinet, I would have to cut the backboard 31½" wide and the bottom board 30¼" wide. All other dimensions remain the same. The door, upper rail and shelf widths would have to change, but they are easily calculated, as you'll see when we construct the cabinet.

FRAMELESS BASE CABINET UPPER RAILS

Frameless base cabinets require an upper rail so the door clears the countertop. For my cabinets, I install a 1½"-high rail as shown in the step-by-step construction details. The height is constant regardless of the cabinet width, and the rail width is equal to the bottom board's width.

CALCULATING THE DOOR SIZE

This method of calculating door size is used when installing full-overlay hidden hinges. Cabinets without a face frame, commonly called frameless style, are best fitted with doors using the hidden hinge. The cabinet box is 31" high with a 1½"-high rail. A 24"-wide cabinet has an inside width of 22¾", and the door, or doors on a double-door cabinet, are 1" wider in total than the interior width. Therefore, you'll need two 11⅞"-wide doors (22¾" + 1" divided by 2).

The door is mounted flush with the bottom surface of the bottom board and overlaps the rail by ½". That means the door height is 30".

I use the 1½"-high rail for a specific reason. As you'll see when using veneer sheet material, the melamine PB rail is replaced with solid wood to match the veneer. The 1½" height is the dressed size of 1×2 boards, so I simply cut my rail lengths from this standard wood size.

Upper frameless cabinets typically have doors that cover the bottom and top board edges. Or stated another way, the door height for uppers is equal to the height of the cabinet side boards.

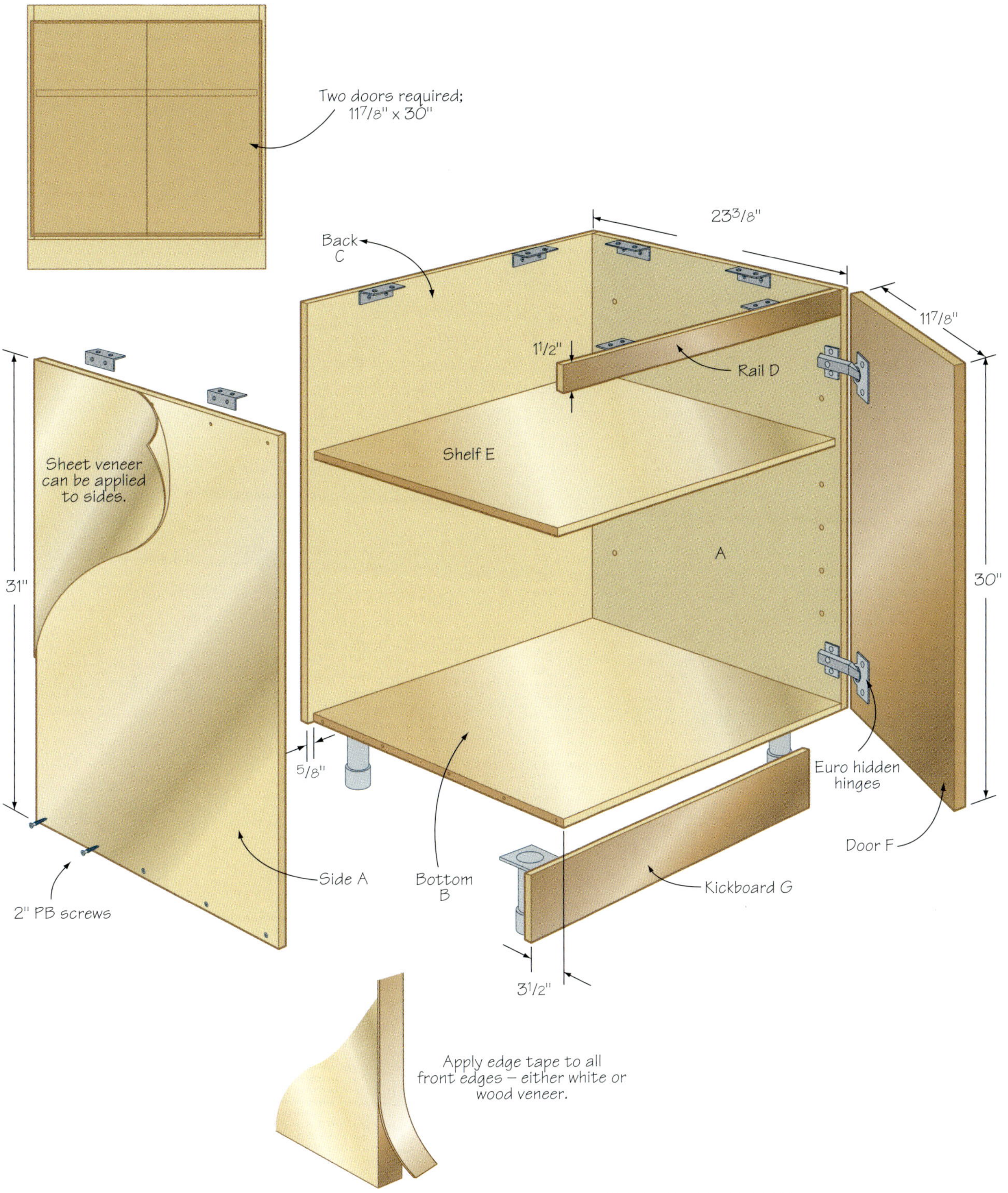

INCHES (MILLIMETERS)

REFERENCE	QUANTITY	PART	STOCK	THICKNESS	(mm)	WIDTH	(mm)	LENGTH	(mm)
A	2	sides	melamine PB	5/8	(16)	23 3/8	(594)	31	(787)
B	1	bottom	melamine PB	5/8	(16)	23 3/8	(594)	22 3/4	(578)
C	1	back	melamine PB	5/8	(16)	24	(610)	31	(787)
D	1	rail	melamine PB	5/8	(16)	1 1/2	(38)	22 3/4	(578)
E	1	shelf	melamine PB	5/8	(16)	22 11/16	(576)	23 3/8	(594)
F	2	doors	melamine PB	5/8	(16)	11 7/8	(302)	30	(762)
G	1	kickboard G	melamine PB	5/8	(16)	4 1/4	(108)	24	(610)

HARDWARE & SUPPLIES

- 4–cabinet legs
- 8–countertop clips
- 2" (51mm) PB screws
- 5/8" (16mm) screws
- 4–hinges
- white melamine iron-on edge tape
- toe kickboard clips
- shelf pins

Building a 24" Frameless Base

1 Cut all the parts as detailed in the materials list. Drill holes for the adjustable shelf pins. These holes can be drilled using a homemade jig such as the one I'm using. It's a piece of flat metal mounted on two $\frac{3}{4}$" blocks that are $31\frac{1}{16}$" apart. Shelf hole spacing is a matter of personal taste, and I normally space holes about $1\frac{1}{4}$" (32mm) on center.

2 Apply iron-on edge tape to the exposed edges of the sides A and bottom B, to the underside of the rail D and the front edge of shelf E. The easiest tape to apply is heat activated with an iron. Use an inexpensive hand trimmer to remove the excess tape on the sides.

3 Secure the sides A to the bottom B. Use 2" screws that are designed for particleboard joinery. Space the screws 6" apart and always predrill and countersink the screw hole. The back C is attached with 2"-long PB screws at 6" centers. The back C should be flush with the bottom edge of the bottom B and flush with the outside edges of the sides A. This board will strengthen and square the cabinet.

4 Secure the rail D to the base cabinet, using 2" screws. Install two screws per side in predrilled pilot holes. The rail should be flush with the front edges of the sides A and even with the top edges.

5 Attach four adjustable cabinet legs so part of the flange supports the sides A. The back legs are installed on each back corner and the front legs are attached $3\frac{1}{2}$" back from the front edge. Use $\frac{5}{8}$"-long screws through the leg flanges to secure them to the cabinet. Adjustable legs come in various styles and are attached using different methods. However, the legs shown here are commonly used in the kitchen and bathroom cabinet industry. If you prefer, you can build and attach a fixed base (plinth) that's $4\frac{1}{4}$" high.

6 Install eight countertop clips, two per inside face, on the sides A, back C and rail D. These are secured with $^5/_8$" PB screws. They will be used to attach the countertop.

7 Apply white iron-on edge tape to the edges of the doors F. Drill two 35mm holes in each door, $^1/_8$" back from the door edge and 4" on center from the bottom and top. These holes will be used to attach the hidden hinges.

8 Screw the hinges in place with the cabinet hinge plate attached. I am using Blum 107° clip-on full-overlay hinges on my cabinet. The hinge is properly installed when it's at 90° to the door's edge. Use a square to align the hinge while inserting the screws.

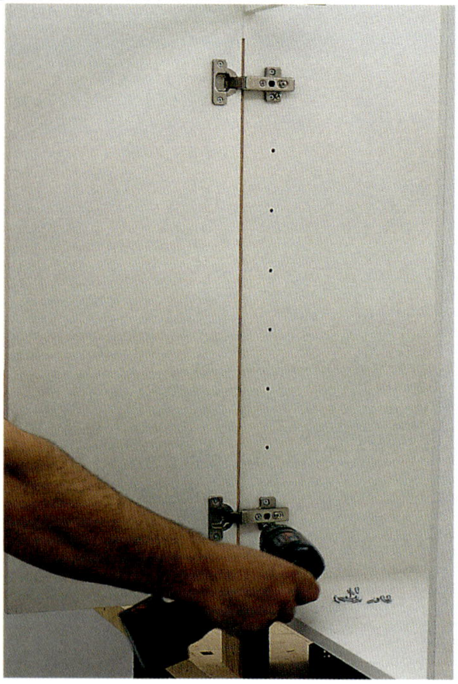

9 It's easy to guarantee perfect door placement using the simple installation method detailed in chapter one. However, I'll review the steps. First, cut a $\frac{1}{8}$" thick spacer, which is nothing more than a strip of wood. Then, place the door in its correct open position, making sure the vertical alignment is correct. The spacer strip is placed between the door and cabinet side edge. Insert screws through the hinge plate and into the cabinet side board. After both hinges are secured, remove the door from the hinge plates and install the screws in the plate that is hidden by the hinge. Reinstall the doors and adjust if necessary. Notice that I've placed a block under the cabinet. The cabinet bottom and door rest on this block so the door will be held flush with the lower face edge of the bottom board while I attach the door.

10 A kickboard G can be installed after the cabinet is secured in place. If this is a stand alone cabinet, you should inset the legs $3\frac{1}{2}$" on each side. If the cabinet is in a run of cabinets, you have to inset only the outside units to secure the kick-board. Attach toe kickboard clips to the kickboard. These metal clips slip on the leg shafts and hold the board securely.

11 The finishing touches for this cabinet are dependent on its intended use. A standard rolled-edge countertop can be attached, or a custom countertop, such as the one detailed earlier in this chapter can be installed. The screws can be hidden with a number of screw cover caps, such as the white ones shown or stick-on white dots. If the cabinet sides will be visible, the white melamine can be covered with veneer or a panel matching the door style can be installed. If you use veneer sheet material and want hidden fasteners, consider using the biscuit method of joinery that was discussed in chapter one.

Veneered Utility Cabinets

Hundreds of veneers are available – everything from the simple preglued white edge tape to large sheets of real wood. Applying wood veneer to the front edges and exposed sides of a cabinet will give it the appearance of a wood cabinet once matching doors are installed. The doors can be wood or veneer-covered particleboard.

Prior to assembling the cabinet as previously detailed, apply wood edge tape to the front edges of the sides and bottom instead of the white melamine edge tape. Trimming some of the wood veneers, such as oak, can be tricky because the trimmer tends to follow the grain and rip the tape. To solve this problem, I use a router with a flush-trim bit and lightly sand the edge. Some of the other woods, like maple and birch, don't have the open grain pattern and are easier to trim. However, I always use a flush-trim bit with wood veneers for a nice clean edge. And in place of the 1½"-high melamine PB rail, I install a solid-wood rail to match the veneer and doors.

CONSTRUCTION NOTES

If the cabinet will be a freestanding unit, use screw cover caps and tape the back's side edges. Install a piece of rolled-edge countertop that is available at the home center and you'll have the ideal laundry room cabinet.

A wood base can be used in place of the adjustable cabinet legs. The base frame is usually 4¼" high so the base, cabinet and countertop thickness total 36" in height.

This utility cabinet is a great addition to the workshop or a hobby room. Or you may need extra storage in the basement for that winemaking hobby. It's a useful and versatile unit.

I have made a few of these utility cabinets with wheels attached in place of the cabinet legs. They are useful in the workshop as mobile tables and great for mounting drill presses and other small power tools.

This style of cabinet has dozens of uses. It's strong and self-supporting because of the modular style and ⅝" thick back. Add a drawer, more shelves, some pullouts or wheels to solve many of those storage problems around your home. And best of all, you can make it any width you need.

Drawer Requirements

If you plan to add a drawer in the base cabinet, an additional rail is required. The amount of drawer height is dependent on the rail position. I always add 1" to my drawer height when determining the lower rail position. For example, if I needed a 5"- high drawer, I would install the lower rail 6" below the upper rail. In the case of veneered cabinets, the rail is solid wood or veneer-faced PB.

It's also necessary to adjust the door height when adding a drawer. Using a standard utility cabinet with 31" sides as an example, I would need a 22½"-high door and a 7"-high drawer face. The space between the doors and drawer face is ½" in the center of the bottom rail.

Notice that adding the door height to the drawer face height, plus the space, equals a total of 30". That's an important dimension when you have a full-door cabinet beside a drawer-over-door cabinet. The door bottoms are at the same position on each cabinet, and the top edge of the drawer is in line with the top edge of the door on the full-door cabinet.

That visual alignment is necessary when a number of cabinets are installed side by side.

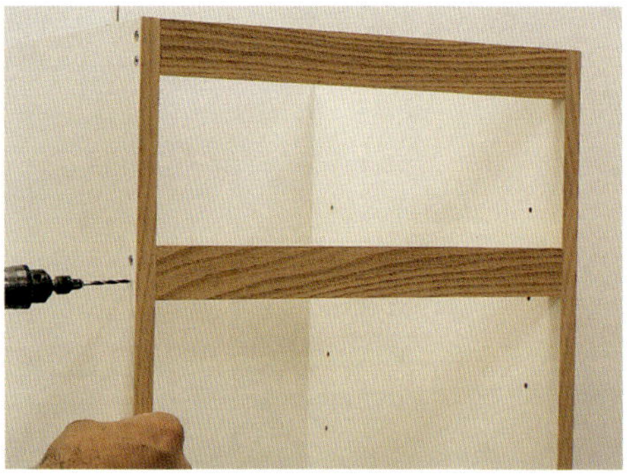

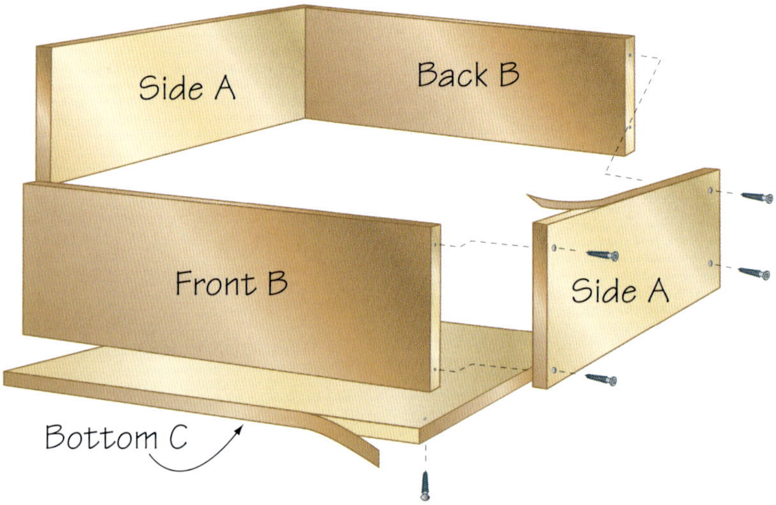

INCHES (MILLIMETERS)

REFERENCE	QUANTITY	PART	STOCK	THICKNESS	(mm)	WIDTH	(mm)	LENGTH	(mm)
A	2	sides	PB	5/8	(16)	4 3/8	(111)	22	(559)
B	2	front/back	PB	5/8	(16)	21 3/4	(552)	22	(559)
C	1	bottom	PB	5/8	(16)	4 3/8	(111)	20 1/2	(521)

HARDWARE & SUPPLIES

iron-on edge tape
2" (51mm) PB screws
plastic screw cover caps
drawer glides

Building Drawers for a Base Cabinet

1 Cut the drawer parts. My cabinet width is 24", so my drawer width is 24" less the side thicknesses (2 @ $\frac{5}{8}$" = $1\frac{1}{4}$"), and the $\frac{1}{2}$" space per side required for the drawer glide hardware, or $21\frac{3}{4}$" wide. The drawer will be 22" deep.

2 Use iron-on edge tape and cover the top edges of the drawer sides, front and back, as well as the sides of the bottom. Trim the edge tape with an edge trimmer or sharp chisel.

3 Secure the drawer sides A to the front and back B with 2"-long PB screws.

4 The exposed screw heads should be driven flush with the melamine surface and covered with plastic screw cover caps. Another option for covering screw heads is the new self-adhesive cover dots. Both are available at most woodworking stores, and the cover dots are also available in wood veneer to match any of the sheet veneers – so you're not restricted to white melamine particleboard.

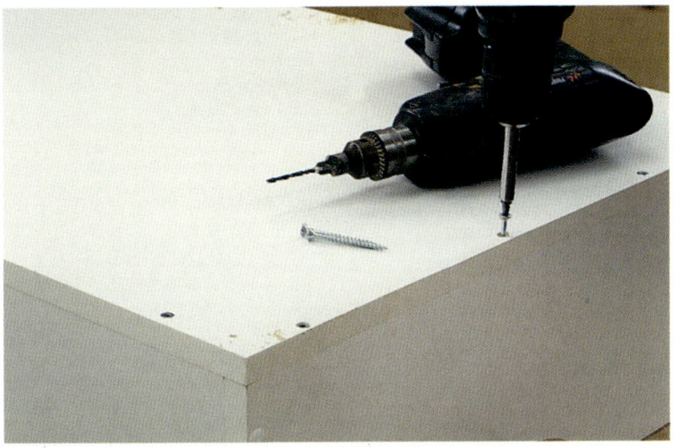

5 Attach the bottom C with 2" PB screws about 6" apart. If the bottom has been cut accurately, the drawer box will be square.

6 Attach the drawer glides according to the manufacturer's instructions. Take your time aligning the drawer glides, making sure they are at 90° to the cabinet's front edge. This step demands a certain amount of accuracy or the drawer will not operate properly.

shop talk | ***Building Pullouts***

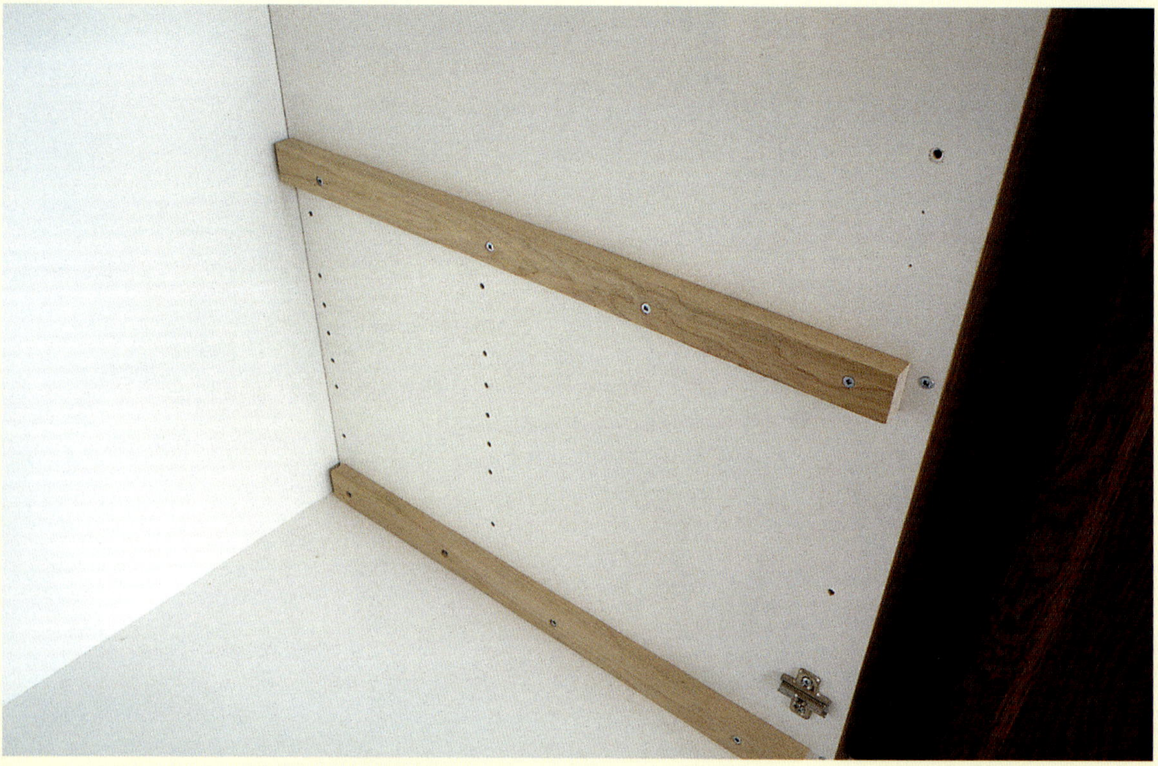

You can install pullout shelves or drawers, behind doors, in base cabinets. They are easily accessible and offer a number of advantages over the traditional shelf.

Drawers installed behind doors are constructed following the steps previously detailed and use the same drawer guide hardware. However, the hardware is mounted on ¾"-thick hardwood or ⅝"-thick melamine PB cleats. This is necessary so the drawer will clear the cabinet doors. Normally, cleats are mounted on the hinge side of the cabinet, so a single-door cabinet needs cleats only on the hinge side. A two-door cabinet must have cleats on both side panels.

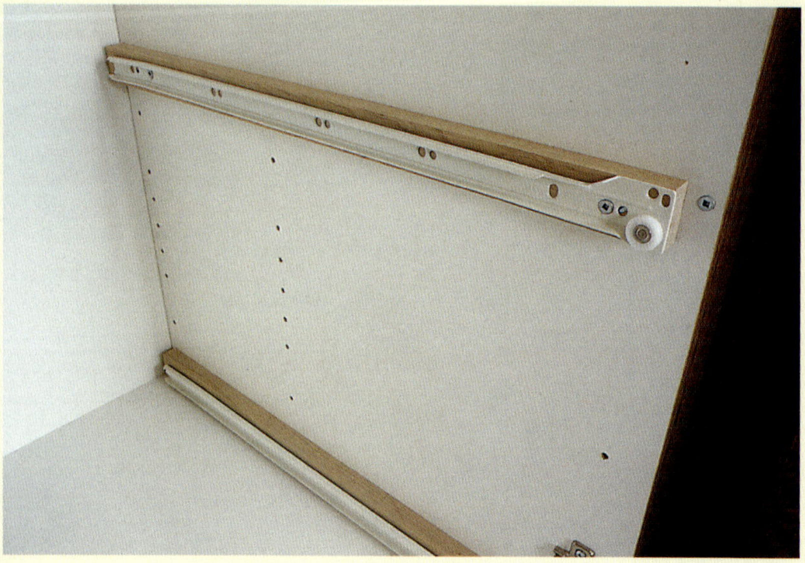

I'm using ⅝"-thick melamine-coated particleboard for my pullout shelves or drawers. Using the previous cabinet example size of a 24"-wide, double-door cabinet, it will now be necessary to account for the cleat thickness on each side, as well as the space required for the drawer glide hardware. My pullout shelf or drawer width will therefore be 20¼" wide using ¾" thick hardwood cleats. The pullout width is calculated by using the interior cabinet width of 22¾" (the cabinet is built with ⅝"-thick sheet material), subtracting the thicknesses of two ¾" cleats as well as the required drawer glide hardware clearance of 1".

PROJECT 3

utility wall cabinets

Utility wall cabinets can be used for many applications. Install them in the laundry room over the washer and dryer, on a garage wall, in the workshop or even in the basement to gain a little extra storage room. Wall cabinets help you to organize and recover valuable unused space. And best of all, they're simple and inexpensive to build.

A wall cabinet can be made entirely from ⅝" melamine particleboard (PB). A 4' × 8' sheet will cost about $30 but will provide enough material for two cabinets, including the doors.

Wood veneer can be applied to the exterior surfaces of the melamine PB cabinet to match the décor of any room, or you can use any of the plywood or particleboard veneer sheets. A simple flat-panel door can be made from veneer sheet goods, or a more traditional five-piece door can be used.

Cabinet Sizes and Styles

Frameless-style wall cabinets are simple to build, and any size, to fit in a particular space, can be assembled. The following chart shows the board sizes for standard cabinets constructed with ⅝"-thick material, but I'll explain how to calculate cabinet part dimensions for any cabinet you require.

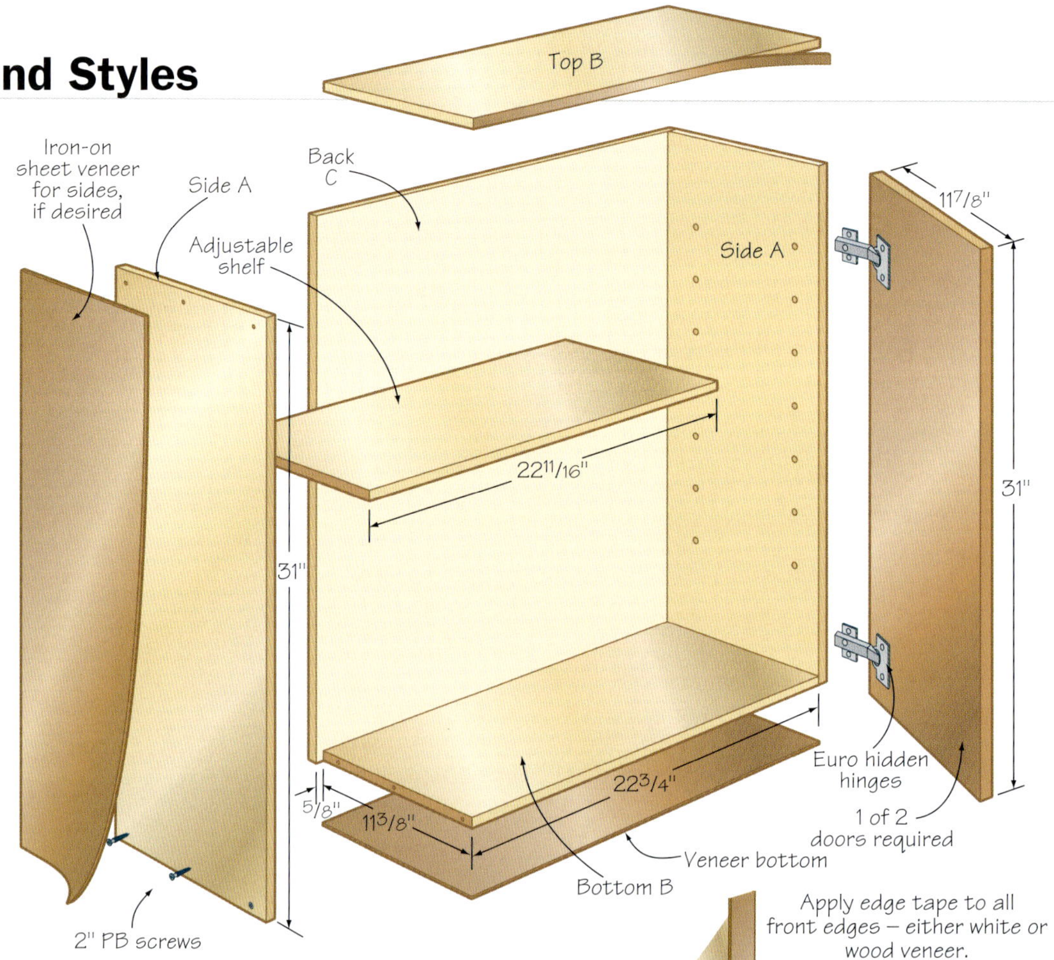

cabinet parts list

CABINET WIDTH	TWO SIDES A D x H	ONE BOTTOM & TOP B D x W	ONE BACK C W x H
12" (305mm)	11⅜" x 31" (305mm x 787mm)	11⅜" x 10¾" (289mm x 273mm)	12" x 31" (305mm x 787mm)
15" (381mm)	11⅜" x 31" (305mm x 787mm)	11⅜" x 13¾" (289mm x 349mm)	15" x 31" (381mm x 787mm)
18" (457mm)	11⅜" x 31" (305mm x 787mm)	11⅜" x 16¾" (289mm x 425mm)	18" x 31" (457mm x 787mm)
21" (533mm)	11⅜" x 31" (305mm x 787mm)	11⅜" x 19¾" (289mm x 502mm)	21" x 31" (533mm x 787mm)
24" (610mm)	11⅜" x 31" (305mm x 787mm)	11⅜" x 22¾" (289mm x 578mm)	24" x 31" (610mm x 787mm)
27" (686mm)	11⅜" x 31" (305mm x 787mm)	11⅜" x 25¾" (289mm x 654mm)	27" x 31" (686mm x 787mm)
30" (762mm)	11⅜" x 31" (305mm x 787mm)	11⅜" x 28¾" (289mm x 730mm)	30" x 31" (762mm x 787mm)
33" (838mm)	11⅜" x 31" (305mm x 787mm)	11⅜" x 31¾" (289mm x 806mm)	33" x 31" (838mm x 787mm)
36" (914mm)	11⅜" x 31" (305mm x 787mm)	11⅜" x 34¾" (289mm x 883mm)	36" x 31" (914mm x 787mm)

1 Cut all the required parts for the width of wall cabinet you want to build and apply edge tape to the exposed, or front edges of the cabinet. Drill holes for the adjustable shelf pins as previously detailed. Attach the sides A to the top and bottom B, using 2" PB screws at 6" centers. As discussed earlier, be sure to drill a pilot hole before installing the screw.

2 Install the back C, using 2" PB screws in piloted holes. The back, when flush with all outside edges, will square the cabinet.

SHOP TIP

Calculating Frameless Wall Cabinet Door Sizes

Frameless wall cabinet door heights are the same as the cabinet side board height. The width, when installing the door(s) using full-overlay hidden hinges, is found by measuring the cabinet's inside dimension and adding 1". A 12"-wide cabinet will require a door that's 11¾" wide by 31" high (10¾" inside width plus 1" using ⅝" material for the case).

When calculating doors for wider cabinets, add 1" to the interior width and divide by two. I wouldn't recommend using a single door when the cabinet is greater than 18" wide. A 24"-wide wall cabinet will need two 11⅞"-wide by 31"-high doors, using the same formula.

3 Cut the shelf boards. They are normally as deep as the bottom and 1⁄16" narrower. I sometimes use construction adhesive and a 5⁄8" plastic cap moulding for the front edge of the shelf to add protection where most of the bumps can occur. This tight-fitting moulding is available at all building centers. As I did for the base cabinets, I'm using 3⁄16" plastic and steel shelf pins in the previously drilled holes to support my shelves.

4 Cut the door, using the formula discussed previously, and install it using the same procedures that were detailed for the base cabinet project. All that's left to do is to attach the cabinet to the wall studs using 3" wood screws through the backboard.

SHOP TIP

Calculating Non-Standard Size Cabinets

When you need a specific-size cabinet, calculate the part sizes based on the cabinet width you require. I will use 5⁄8"-thick melamine PB for this project.

For example, I need a 23¾"-wide cabinet over my clothes dryer and I want it 18" deep. My cabinet side boards will be 17⅜" deep by 31" high. The top and bottom boards will be equal to the total cabinet width minus the side board thickness, or 17⅜" deep by 22½" wide. My backboard is 23¾" wide by 31" high. And using the door calculation formula for full-overlay hidden hinges I will need two doors, each 11¾" wide by 31" high.

PROJECT 4

basic bookcase construction

This bookcase can be used in any room. It would be perfect in a child's room for displaying awards and collectibles, in the family room for pictures and books, in the kitchen for a cookbook collection or even in the basement for added storage. The material I used is secondary to the construction steps; you can use any sheet goods or solid wood that matches your décor.

This project was constructed using solid knotty pine. The material is standard 1×8 lumber attached with simple butt joints. The doors are raised-panel tongue and groove made on a table saw. However, if you don't have a saw, you can buy ready-made doors or use glued-up panels from the home store. Hidden hinges were used to mount the doors. However, if you don't own a drill press and a 35mm-hinge boring bit, many other hinges can be used.

I've used basic joinery and fasteners to complete this project – the butt joint with screws and glue. Counterbore the screw holes and fill them with wood plugs. It's a strong joint that looks great and is easy to do.

If you're more experienced and feel comfortable with advanced joinery procedures, you can use biscuits, dowels or dado joints. Anyone can build this case with simple or involved joinery. Have fun building this project. You'll find it extremely useful, and the person lucky enough to get this bookcase will appreciate your efforts.

The plans for this case can be altered to suit your specific needs. Make it deeper using 1×12 stock, build it higher or wider, use premade doors or no doors at all; the options are endless.

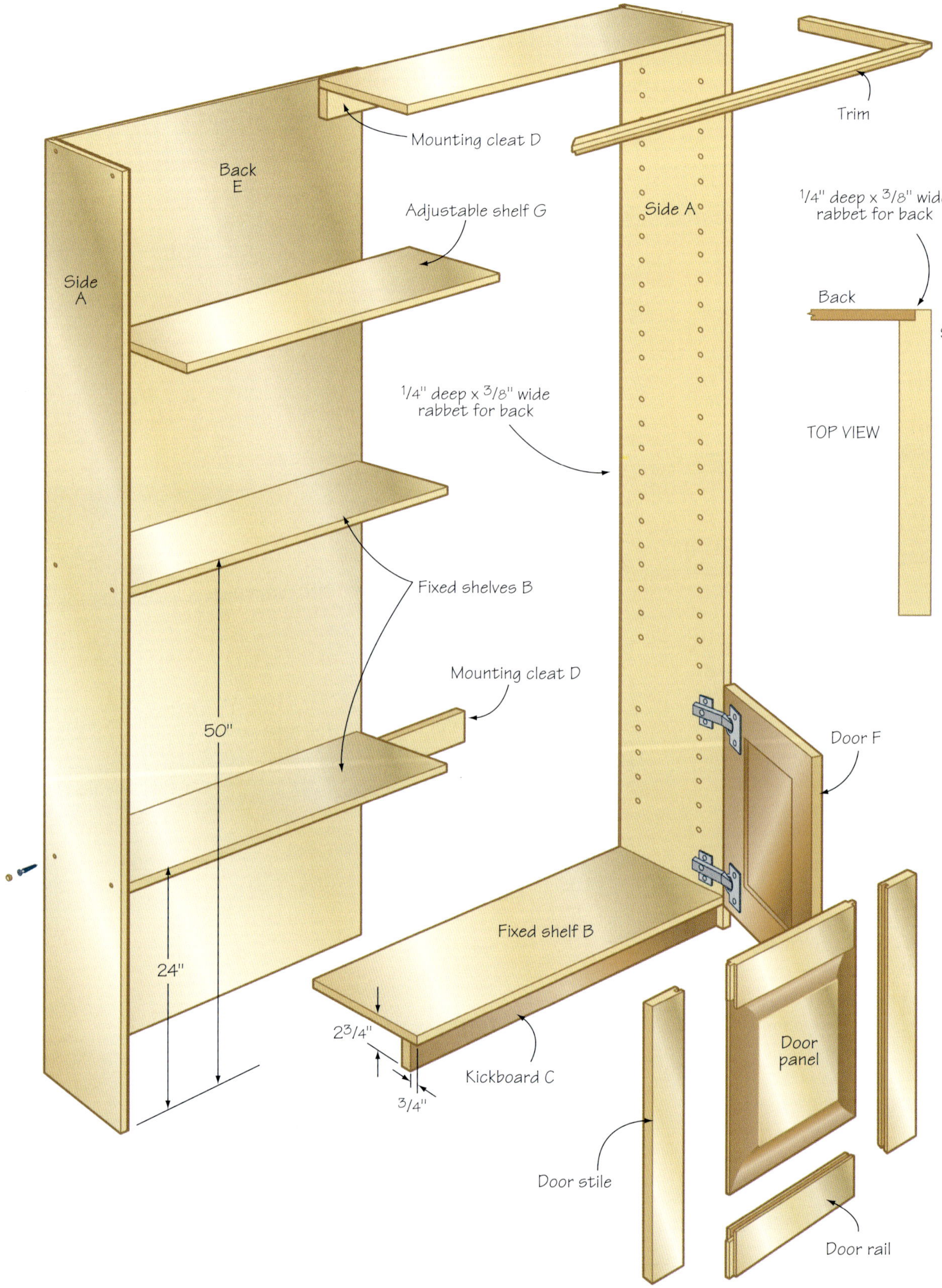
Trim
Mounting cleat D
Back
E
Adjustable shelf G
Side A
Side
A
1/4" deep x 3/8" wide
rabbet for back
Back
Side
1/4" deep x 3/8" wide
rabbet for back
TOP VIEW
Fixed shelves B
Mounting cleat D
50"
Door F
24"
Fixed shelf B
2 3/4"
Kickboard C
3/4"
Door
panel
Door stile
Door rail

1 Cut the sides A to the dimensions listed. Rabbet both back inside faces of the side boards 1/4" deep by 3/8" wide. (If you don't have the equipment to rabbet the sides, cut the veneer plywood back E 36" wide, and later you'll nail and glue this board to the back edges of the sides. Also, cut the fixed shelves B 7 1/4" deep if you don't cut a rabbet on the side panels.)

2 Cut the four fixed shelves B 7" deep if you are installing the back E in rabbets on the sides A. Attach one fixed shelf at the top and the other three at 2 3/4", 24" and 50" from the bottom edge of side A, as shown in the illustration. Use 2" wood screws in counterbored holes and fill with wood plugs.

INCHES (MILLIMETERS)

REFERENCE	QUANTITY	PART	STOCK	THICKNESS	(mm)	WIDTH	(mm)	LENGTH	(mm)	COMMENTS
A	2	sides	pine	3/4	(19)	7 1/4	(184)	84	(2134)	
B	4	fixed shelves	pine	3/4	(19)	7	(178)	34 1/2	(876)	
C	1	kickboard	pine	3/4	(19)	2	(51)	34 1/2	(876)	
D	2	mounting cleats	pine	3/4	(19)	2	(51)	34 1/2	(876)	
E	1	back	veneer ply	1/4	(6)	35 1/4	(895)	82	(2083)	
F	2	doors	pine	3/4	(19)	17 3/4	(451)	21 3/4	(552)	See "Table Saw Frame & Raised-Panel Door" at the end of this project.
G	6	adjustable shelves	pine	3/4	(19)	6 3/4	(171)	34 7/16	(875)	
H		trim moulding	pine			22 11/16	(576)	5ft.	(1.5m)	

HARDWARE & SUPPLIES

2"-(51mm) wood screws
glue
wood plugs
1" (25mm) finishing nails or brads
shelf pins
4-hidden hinges
2-door handles

SHOP TIP

Using Dowels

Dowel joinery is another popular method used to join boards. Prior to the now common biscuit joint, it was used in furniture shops as the connector of choice. A dowel is a long piece of wood that fits into drilled holes on either board. Alignment is critical, so most woodworkers use center plugs to align the holes.

3 Install the kickboard C under the bottom shelf. Set it back ¾" from the front edge of the case. Use glue and 2" wood screws through each side A.

4 This shallow case should be anchored to the wall. Install two mounting cleats D, one under the 24"-high shelf and the other under the top shelf. Install screws from the sides and through the fixed shelves.

5 Attach the back E with glue and 1" finishing nails or brad nails. The 35¼"-wide back will fit into the side board rabbets. If you choose not to cut the rabbets, make the back 36" wide.

6 Round over all the front edges of the case but leave the top fixed shelf straight so the trim moulding will sit flat. Use a ¼" roundover bit in a router or ease the edges by hand with sandpaper.

7 Select a moulding and attach it to the top with glue and finishing nails. Countersink the nail heads and fill the holes with wood putty. The moulding style isn't critical, so choose one that suits your taste. Install it flush with the bottom edge of the top fixed shelf. Cut as many adjustable shelf boards as needed for your display case. Round over the front edge of each shelf board with a router or sandpaper.

8 The shelf holes are drilled using a simple jig made from scrap lumber. Shelf pins are available in many styles. Select a style suitable for your case and drill the appropriate-size holes.

shop talk | *Table Saw Frame & Raised Panel Door*

If you plan to install doors on the lower section, you'll need two doors $17\frac{3}{4}$" wide by $21\frac{3}{4}$" high. They are attached with hidden hinges and are aligned flush with the lower edge of the bottom fixed shelf. The doors can be made from flat glued-up panels that are available at the local lumber store. Or you can make elegant raised-panel doors on a table saw.

1 Cut four stiles at $\frac{3}{4}$" thick by $2\frac{1}{4}$" wide by $21\frac{3}{4}$" long and four rails at $\frac{3}{4}$" by $2\frac{1}{4}$" by $14\frac{3}{4}$" long. The rail size is found by subtracting the stile widths from the total door width ($17\frac{3}{4}$" - $4\frac{1}{2}$" = $13\frac{1}{4}$") and adding the two tenon lengths of $\frac{3}{4}$" each to the rail length ($13\frac{1}{4}$" + $1\frac{1}{2}$" = $14\frac{3}{4}$"). Use the table saw and make a groove $\frac{1}{4}$" wide by $\frac{3}{4}$" deep on one edge of each rail and stile. Center the groove on each edge.

2 The rails require a $\frac{1}{4}$"-thick by $\frac{3}{4}$"-long tenon centered on each end of both rails. Use the table saw and a regular blade to make the tenons. Make the shoulder cut first and then nibble the waste material toward the end of each rail.

3 The inside dimension of my frame is $13\frac{1}{4}$" wide by $17\frac{1}{4}$" high. My panel will be $14\frac{11}{16}$" wide by $18\frac{11}{16}$" high so it will fit in the grooves with a little room for movement. Glue up $\frac{3}{4}$"-thick boards a little wider and longer than required, then trim to the finished size. Now use the table saw to score each panel $\frac{1}{8}$" deep and 2" in from each edge as shown.

SHOP TIP

A solid $\frac{3}{4}$"-thick panel is required for each door. If you have an accurately tuned table saw and a biscuit joiner, you can make your own edge-glued panels as detailed in Chapter 1, page 16. These panels can also be made without biscuits by simply edge-gluing boards. You can also purchase glued panels at most local home stores or lumberyards.

4 Tip the saw blade 10° away from the fence. I have extended the height of my fence to give better control when cutting high panels. It's a nice feature and can be easily made with a few boards. Set the fence to cut a $^3/_{16}$" edge on the door. That will give the correct taper and the panel will sit in the frame grooves. The blade height is set slightly below the score on the panel.

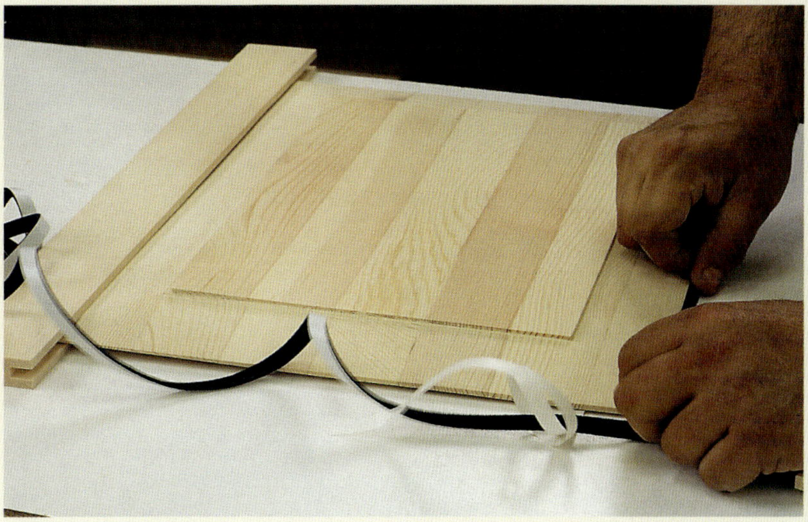

5 Sand the raised section of your panel with a large flat sanding block. Assemble the door, using glue on the tenons only; do not glue the panel. To stop door rattling, place small strips of foam in the grooves before inserting the panel. The foam strips I use are commonly sold in hardware stores as door weather strip. It comes in long lengths, which can be cut, and is an inexpensive way to stop center panel rattles.

6 Drill two 35mm holes in each door for the hidden hinges. Refer to the instructions earlier in this chapter when you are ready to install the doors with hidden hinges.

shop talk **notes**

Hidden hinges require a 35mm hole. But if you don't have a drill press, other hinges can be used. Many surface-mounted types are available that operate much like the hidden hinge. Purchase the hinges before you make the doors.

The stiles and rails can be prepared as previously described, and a $^1/_4$"-thick veneer-covered plywood panel can be used in place of the solid raised-panel door. This is called a frame-and-flat-panel door. It's a low-cost option, and it looks great.

Flat-panel doors have $^1/_4$"-thick plywood center panels, so they are always lower than the surface of the frame. Raised-panel doors use solid-wood panels that have their edges milled. The panel face can be lower or on the same plane as the frame facing. You can control the panel position by deciding on the frame and panel thicknesses before starting to build a door.

To make a door with the raised-panel top surface on the same level as the frame members, use $^3/_4$"-thick frame boards with a $^1/_2$"-thick panel that fits in a groove that is cut $^1/_4$" in from the back face of the frame members. Or you can use a combination of $^7/_8$"-thick frame pieces with a $^5/_8$"-thick panel set $^1/_4$" in from the back face of the frame members.

If you want the panel face raised above the frame member front faces, use the same thickness frame and panel pieces. It's a style choice that you can decide on after making a few sample doors.

rustic pine chest of drawers | *page 48*

child's storage bed | *page 54*

Children's Bedroom Furniture

student's work center | *page 59*

This chapter is devoted to building practical bedroom furniture projects for children. Their rooms are often small, so using space wisely is the focus of this section.

Bedrooms are intended for sleeping, so a bed with a matching chest of drawers to organize clothes is included. However, I can't guarantee the chest of drawers will make children stop using the floor as their clothing storage area! There is also a student's work center for study time.

A "Shop Talk" section deals with traditional-style drawer construction, which is commonly found in rustic or country pine furniture.

I used solid pine and oak veneer sheet material for these projects because it was the material that suited my requirements. However, any solid wood or sheet material can be used for any or all of the projects, so use the material you prefer.

PROJECT 1

rustic pine chest of drawers

This rustic pine chest is easy to build. With five large drawers, it can hold a great deal of clothing. The chest is a low-cost solution to organizing a child's bedroom. But don't stop with the chest; it's only the beginning. A matching dresser and armoire can be easily built in the same style by altering a few dimensions.

Traditional, country or rustic pine furniture is simplicity at its best. The drawers are solid wood with an applied drawer front. They slide on wood frames that — with a little paste wax applied once a year — work very well. No fancy hardware here, just solid wood.

The top and sides are glued-up ¾"- thick pine boards. The techniques for creating these panels are described in chapter 1, page 16. I'm using #1 and #2 pine, which is relatively inexpensive.

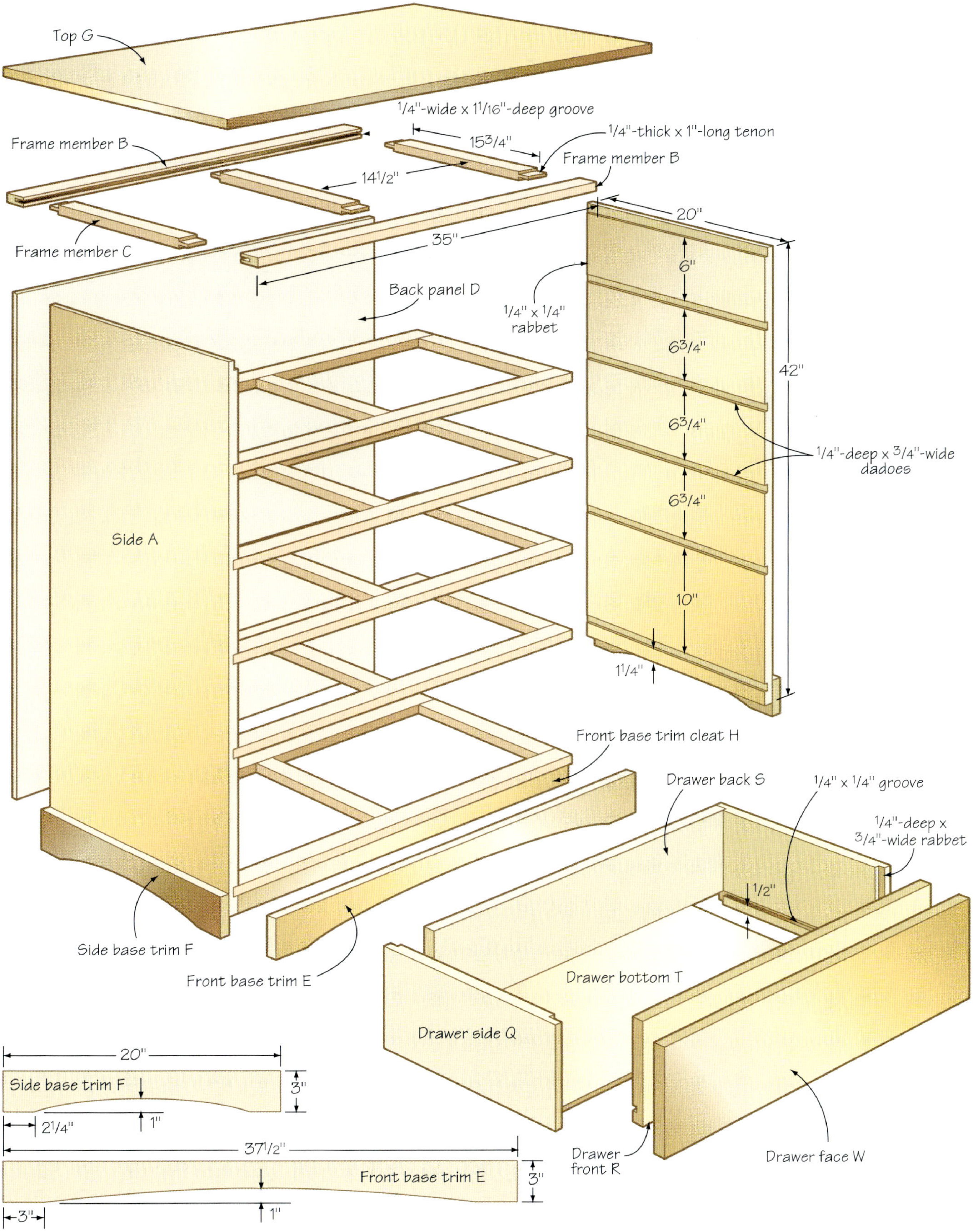
Top G
1/4"-wide x 1 1/16"-deep groove
Frame member B
15 3/4"
1/4"-thick x 1"-long tenon
Frame member B
14 1/2"
Frame member C
35"
20"
Back panel D
6"
1/4" x 1/4" rabbet
6 3/4"
42"
6 3/4"
1/4"-deep x 3/4"-wide dadoes
6 3/4"
Side A
10"
1 1/4"
Front base trim cleat H
Drawer back S
1/4" x 1/4" groove
1/4"-deep x 3/4"-wide rabbet
1/2"
Side base trim F
Front base trim E
Drawer bottom T
Drawer side Q
20"
Side base trim F
3"
2 1/4"
1"
37 1/2"
Drawer front R
Drawer face W
Front base trim E
3"
3"
1"

Building the Chest

1 Glue up and cut the two sides A to a finished size of $\frac{3}{4}$" thick by 20" wide by 42" high. Follow the procedures in "Making Solid-Wood Panel Glue-Ups" detailed in chapter 1, page 16. Use a stacked carbide-tipped dado cutter to form the dadoes as well as the back rabbets on the inside face of each side panel. The dadoes are all $\frac{3}{4}$" wide and $\frac{1}{4}$" deep. The rabbet to receive the plywood back panel D is also $\frac{1}{4}$" deep, but it has to be only $\frac{1}{4}$" wide. If you don't have a dado blade on your table saw, use a router and straight $\frac{3}{4}$" cutting bit. The rabbet can also be completed with this straight bit, but you should have a guide system to limit the width to $\frac{1}{4}$".

INCHES (MILLIMETERS)

REFERENCE	QUANTITY	PART	STOCK	THICKNESS	(mm)	WIDTH	(mm)	LENGTH	(mm)
A	2	sides	solid wood	$\frac{3}{4}$	(19)	20	(508)	42	(1067)
B	12	frame members	solid wood	$\frac{3}{4}$	(19)	2	(51)	35	(889)
C	18	frame members	solid wood	$\frac{3}{4}$	(19)	2	(51)	$17\frac{3}{4}$	(451)
D	1	back panel	plywood	$\frac{1}{4}$	(6)	35	(889)	41	(1041)
E	1	front base trim	solid wood	$\frac{3}{4}$	(19)	3	(76)	$37\frac{1}{2}$	(953)
F	2	side base trim	solid wood	$\frac{3}{4}$	(19)	3	(76)	20	(508)
G	1	top	solid wood	$\frac{3}{4}$	(19)	21	(533)	38	(965)
H	1	front base trim cleat	solid wood	$\frac{3}{4}$	(19)	$1\frac{1}{4}$	(32)	$34\frac{1}{2}$	(876)
J	2	drawer sides	solid wood	$\frac{3}{4}$	(19)	$5\frac{7}{8}$	(149)	$19\frac{1}{2}$	(495)
K	1	drawer front	solid wood	$\frac{3}{4}$	(19)	$5\frac{7}{8}$	(149)	$33\frac{3}{8}$	(848)
L	1	drawer back	solid wood	$\frac{3}{4}$	(19)	$5\frac{1}{8}$	(130)	$33\frac{3}{8}$	(848)
M	6	drawer sides	solid wood	$\frac{3}{4}$	(19)	$6\frac{5}{8}$	(168)	$19\frac{1}{2}$	(495)
N	3	drawer fronts	solid wood	$\frac{3}{4}$	(19)	$6\frac{5}{8}$	(168)	$33\frac{3}{8}$	(848)
P	3	drawer backs	solid wood	$\frac{3}{4}$	(19)	$5\frac{7}{8}$	(149)	$33\frac{3}{8}$	(848)
Q	2	drawer sides	solid wood	$\frac{3}{4}$	(19)	$9\frac{7}{8}$	(251)	$19\frac{1}{2}$	(495)
R	1	drawer front	solid wood	$\frac{3}{4}$	(19)	$9\frac{7}{8}$	(251)	$33\frac{3}{8}$	(848)
S	1	drawer back	solid wood	$\frac{3}{4}$	(19)	$9\frac{1}{8}$	(232)	$33\frac{3}{8}$	(848)
T	5	drawer bottoms	plywood	$\frac{1}{4}$	(6)	19	(483)	$33\frac{3}{8}$	(848)
U	1	drawer face	solid wood	$\frac{3}{4}$	(19)	$6\frac{1}{2}$	(165)	35	(889)
V	3	drawer faces	solid wood	$\frac{3}{4}$	(19)	$7\frac{1}{4}$	(184)	35	(889)
W	1	drawer face	solid wood	$\frac{3}{4}$	(19)	$10\frac{1}{2}$	(267)	35	(889)

HARDWARE & SUPPLIES

glue
brad nails
2" (51mm) screws
$1\frac{1}{4}$" (32mm) screws
wood plugs
finishing nails
drawer pulls

2 Cut all the frame members B and C to the sizes indicated in the materials list. The shorter members require a ¼"-thick by 1"-long by 2"-wide tenon on each end. The long members require a ¼"-wide by 1"-deep groove on one long edge. The grooves, as well as the tenons, can be cut with a dado blade on your table saw. However, both types of cuts can also be made with a standard blade in the saw; it's a little slower but can be done with multiple passes.

3 Build the frames as shown in the illustration. The six frames are the same size and constructed in the same manner. Apply glue to each tenon and slide the tenon into the groove. One short frame member is at either end of the long frame member, and the third rail is in the center. Secure the joints with two small brad nails to provide support while the glue sets.

4 Attach the frame assemblies to the sides A. Use glue and small brad nails to secure the frames in the dado cuts. Frame members can be pinned in place by toenailing. Be careful not to drive the nail through the face of the side panel.

5 The back panel D is glued and nailed into the rabbet on each side A. Nail one side, then check that the cabinet is square by measuring the diagonals. Adjust if necessary, and complete the nailing.

6 The base trim consists of boards E and F, cut to the dimensions shown. Cut the lower arcs in each trim board as shown in the illustration, using a band saw or jigsaw. Sand the trim boards smooth. Before installing the front base trim E, glue the front base trim cleat H under, and at the front edge, of the lower frame. Secure the base trim to the chest, using glue and 1¼" screws from inside the chest case. Note that the 2¼" straight edge on the side base trim butts against the front base trim. The ¾" thickness of the front base trim when added to the side base trim, creates a 3"-wide foot on the front and side faces. The boards are installed 1½" up from the bottom edge of the chest sides. Now, round over the top edge of the trim boards with a ¼" roundover bit in a router. If you don't have a router, ease the edges with sandpaper.

7 Construct a glued-up panel to make the top G. Round over the top and bottom edges of the front and sides with a ⅜" roundover bit. Secure the top with 1¼" screws through the top frame.

shop talk | ***Building Rustic Pine Drawers***

Many styles of drawer mounting hardware are available in today's marketplace. But before all these great solutions, drawers and drawer tracks were made entirely of wood. This early drawer style is used when building rustic or country pine furniture. And if accurately assembled, it is still very functional.

Build the drawer box so it's 1/8" narrower than the opening and 1/8" less in height. The drawer faces are 1/2" wider and taller than the openings.

1 Cut all the drawer parts. The drawer front and sides require a 1/4"-wide by 1/4"-deep groove that begins 1/2" up from the bottom edges. The drawer sides also require a 1/4"-deep rabbet that's 3/4" wide on both ends. The rabbets are on the inside face of each drawer side and will receive the drawer front and back. Attach the sides to the back and front, in the rabbets, with glue and finishing nails. The top edges of all boards are flush with each other. The back's bottom edge should end at the top of the grooves so a bottom plywood panel can be inserted.

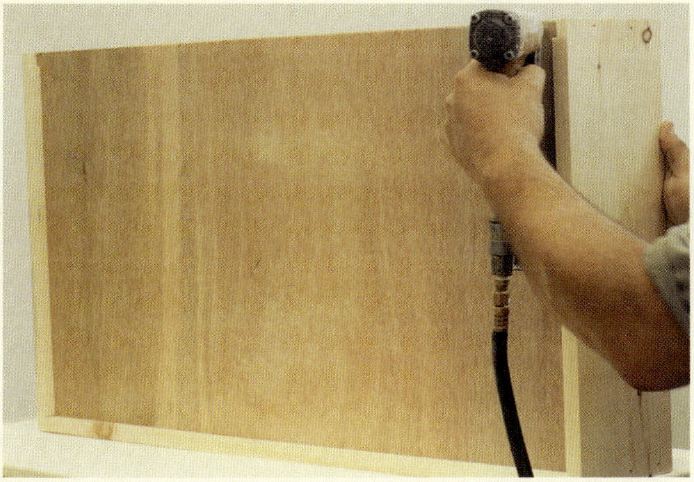

2 From the back of the drawer, slide the 1/4"-thick plywood bottom into the grooves. It should fit snug in the side grooves and go all the way into the front groove. The back's bottom edge will be completely covered when the plywood bottom is seated in the front groove. Nail the bottom board to the back's edge. Do not use glue.

3 Install the drawer box in the cabinet. Round over the front edges of the drawer face and secure it in place. It should overlap the opening by 1/4" on all edges. Attach the face with four 1 1/4" screws through the inside of the drawer box.

PROJECT 2

child's storage bed

This platform storage bed project is a great addition to any child's or teenager's room. It features a bookcase headboard and four large storage drawers.

The bed is built of knotty pine in the rustic or country style. The dimensions given are to accommodate a standard twin mattress measuring 39" wide by 75" long.

I've also detailed a construction method using knockdown hardware. The cap bolts used here can be removed and replaced when the bed is moved.

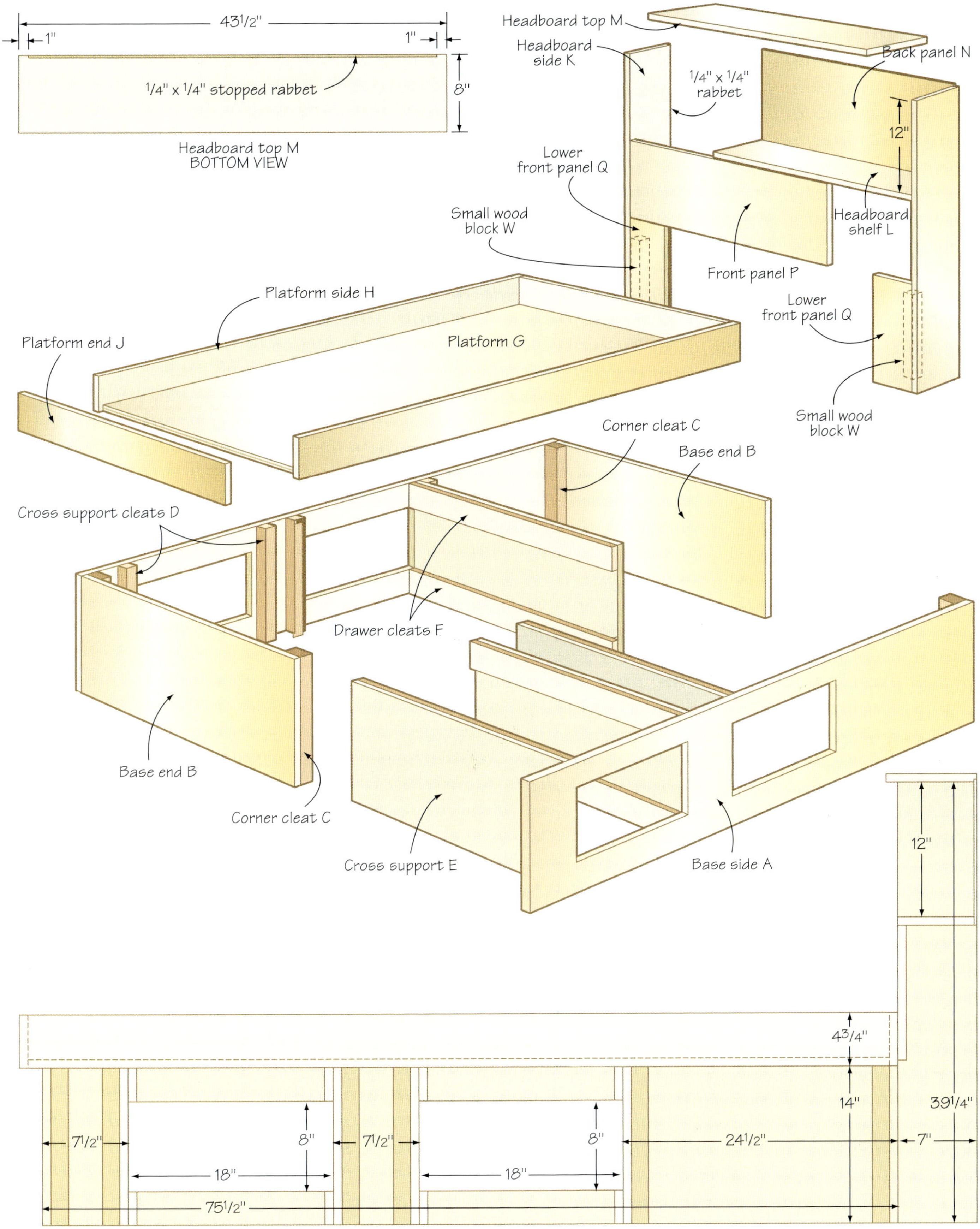

43 1/2"
1"
1"
1/4" x 1/4" stopped rabbet
8"
Headboard top M
BOTTOM VIEW
Headboard top M
Headboard side K
1/4" x 1/4" rabbet
Back panel N
12"
Lower front panel Q
Headboard shelf L
Small wood block W
Front panel P
Platform side H
Lower front panel Q
Platform end J
Platform G
Small wood block W
Corner cleat C
Base end B
Cross support cleats D
Drawer cleats F
Base end B
Corner cleat C
Cross support E
Base side A
12"
4 3/4"
14"
39 1/4"
7 1/2"
8"
7 1/2"
8"
24 1/2"
7"
18"
18"
75 1/2"

INCHES (MILLIMETERS)

REFERENCE	QUANTITY	PART	STOCK	THICKNESS	(mm)	WIDTH	(mm)	LENGTH	(mm)
A	2	base sides	solid wood	3/4	(19)	14	(356)	75 1/2	(1918)
B	2	base ends	solid wood	3/4	(19)	14	(356)	36	(914)
C	4	corner cleats	solid wood	1 1/2	(38)	2 1/4	(57)	14	(356)
D	8	cross support cleats	solid wood	1 1/2	(38)	1 1/2	(38)	14	(356)
E	4	cross supports	plywood	3/4	(19)	14	(356)	36	(914)
F	8	drawer cleats	solid wood	3/4	(19)	3	(76)	36	(914)
G	1	platform	plywood	3/4	(19)	40	(1016)	76	(1930)
H	2	platform sides	solid wood	3/4	(19)	4 3/4	(121)	77 1/2	(1969)
J	2	platform ends	solid wood	3/4	(19)	4 3/4	(121)	40	(1016)
K	2	headboard sides	solid wood	3/4	(19)	7	(178)	39 1/4	(997)
L	1	headboard shelf	solid wood	3/4	(19)	6 3/4	(171)	40	(1016)
M	1	headboard top	solid wood	3/4	(19)	8	(203)	43 1/2	(1105)
N	1	back panel	plywood	1/4	(6)	13	(330)	40 1/2	(1029)
P	1	front panel	solid wood	3/4	(19)	12	(305)	40	(1016)
Q	2	lower front panels	solid wood	3/4	(19)	7 1/4	(184)	14 1/2	(368)
R	8	drawer sides	solid wood	3/4	(19)	7 7/8	(200)	17	(432)
S	4	drawer fronts	solid wood	3/4	(19)	7 7/8	(200)	16 7/8	(429)
T	4	drawer backs	solid wood	3/4	(19)	7 1/8	(181)	16 7/8	(429)
U	4	drawer bottoms	plywood	1/4	(6)	16 1/2	(419)	16 7/8	(429)
V	4	drawer faces	solid wood	3/4	(19)	8 1/2	(216)	18 1/2	(470)
W	2	small wood blocks	solid wood	3/4	(19)	3/4	(19)	12	(305)

HARDWARE & SUPPLIES

glue
2" (51mm) wood screws
cap bolts
1 1/4" (32mm) screws
wood plugs
brad nails
drawer pulls

1 The base sides A and base ends B are two-board glue-ups using pine. I made my panels using stock 1x8 wood and edge-gluing as detailed under "Making Solid Wood Panel Glue-Ups" in chapter 1, page 16. Once the base sides A were glued into a panel and cut to size, I cut out the two drawer openings in each one as shown in the illustration. I could have built the base sides with individual boards, but since it would mean assembling a lot of small pieces to form each base side, this cutout method seemed to be the most practical solution. The base ends B for the bed frame are also two-board glue-ups. Follow the directions on edge-gluing wood, then cut each panel to size and cut out the drawer openings on the base sides with a jigsaw and fine-tooth blade. You can minimize edge chipping with your jigsaw by first using a sharp knife to score the cut lines. Attach the eight cross support cleats D on the inside face of the base sides A. Each cleat is secured with glue and 2" screws, 3/4" back from each drawer opening. Each side of the four openings should have one cleat.

2 Using glue and 2" wood screws, attach the corner cleats C to the inside face of each base end B. The 2 1/4" face of the cleat is installed flush with the outside edge of each base end B. Use knockdown fasteners, called cap bolts, to join the sides A and ends B at each corner. These are easily removed and replaced if the bed has to been taken apart.

3 Four cross supports E will be used to strengthen the base and provide runners for the drawers. The cross supports are ¾"-thick plywood or particleboard, 14" high by 36" wide. Each cross support requires a 3"-high drawer cleat F on the top and bottom to form tracks and top runners for the drawers. Use glue and 1¼" screws to attach the drawer cleats F to the cross supports E.

4 Screw the cross support assemblies to the cross support cleats D with 2" screws. Do not glue these in place, so they can be removed when dismantling the bed. Notice that the drawer cleats face into each drawer space.

5 Cut the plywood platform G, platform sides H and platform ends J as detailed in the materials list. Join the ends J to the platform G, and then attach the sides H. Use glue with 2" wood screws in counterbored holes that are filled with wood plugs. The bottom face of platform G is attached flush with the bottom edges of the sides H and ends J. The overall outside dimension of the frame should be 41½" wide by 77½" long.

6 Secure the mattress platform to the base with 2" screws through the plywood into the corner cleats C. The headboard end of the frame is flush with the base. The sides and footboard end overhang the base by 2". Do not use glue, so the platform can be removed if the bed has to be moved.

7 Cut all the headboard pieces, K, L, M, N, P and Q, as detailed in the materials list. Before beginning the assembly, cut a 1/4"-deep by 1/4"-wide rabbet on the back inside face of the two headboard sides K. Join the sides to the shelf L, 12" down from the top edges of sides K, with glue and 2" wood screws. Install the screws from the outside and fill the counterbored holes with wood plugs.

8 Round over the front and end edges of the top M. Use a 1/4" roundover bit on the top and bottom of each edge. The top also requires a stopped rabbet that's 1/4" wide by 1/4" deep to receive the back panel N. A stopped rabbet is a cut that stops 1" short of the board's ends. This will prevent the rabbet from being seen on the underside of the top at either end. Secure the top M to the sides K with glue and 2" wood screws in plugged holes. Ensure the sides K are spaced 40" apart and the top M extends 1" past each side. The top should overhang the front edge and be aligned flush with the back edges of the sides.

9 Install the 1/4" back panel N with glue and brad nails in the rabbet cuts. The front panel P rests tight to the underside of shelf L. It is secured with glue and 2" wood screws in plugged holes through the sides and shelf. The front panel should be installed flush with the front edges of the sides and shelf.

10 The two lower front panels Q are needed to hide the space between the headboard sides and the base. Join them flush with the front edge of side K and tight to the bottom edge of front panel P. Use 1 1/4" wood screws and glue. I've also used a small wood block W to support the lower top front panel joint. Install this block behind the joint, using glue and screws. Attach the headboard assembly to the base with screws through the back of the lower front panels Q and into the base end B. Build the drawers with panels R, S, T, U and V, following the steps outlined in "Building Rustic Pine Drawers" in this chapter. These drawers will slide on the drawer cleats F.

PROJECT 3

student's work center

Children will work better when they have a dedicated, organized area for their projects and homework. Information and the materials needed to work and study are more effectively used when they are within easy reach. To answer these needs, I've designed a work center that may help get them better organized.

The work center is a desk and hutch combination. It provides space for book storage, three large drawers for supplies, and a large work surface made from high-pressure laminate material. This project was made of solid pine and composite veneer board. It's reasonably easy to build and not very expensive. The finish is polyurethane.

To simplify the building process, look at the components: a three-drawer pedestal, a leg, a desktop and a hutch. I've used pine veneer MDF and solid-wood trim. If the desk is too small or large for your space, change the dimensions. The only major difference between this desk and a wider unit is the hutch width. If you need a 30" × 60" desktop, add the extra width onto the horizontal members of the hutch. And if you do have the space for a deeper desktop, consider building the hutch with 1 × 12 lumber.

This project can be matched to the other furniture in this chapter if it will be in the same room. The drawers in this project track on mechanical glides in place of the traditional wood runners. It can be made with wood runners by duplicating the steps used in the other projects, or the others can use mechanical glides. I used the metal glide option here to illustrate the differences; you can decide on the method that works best for you.

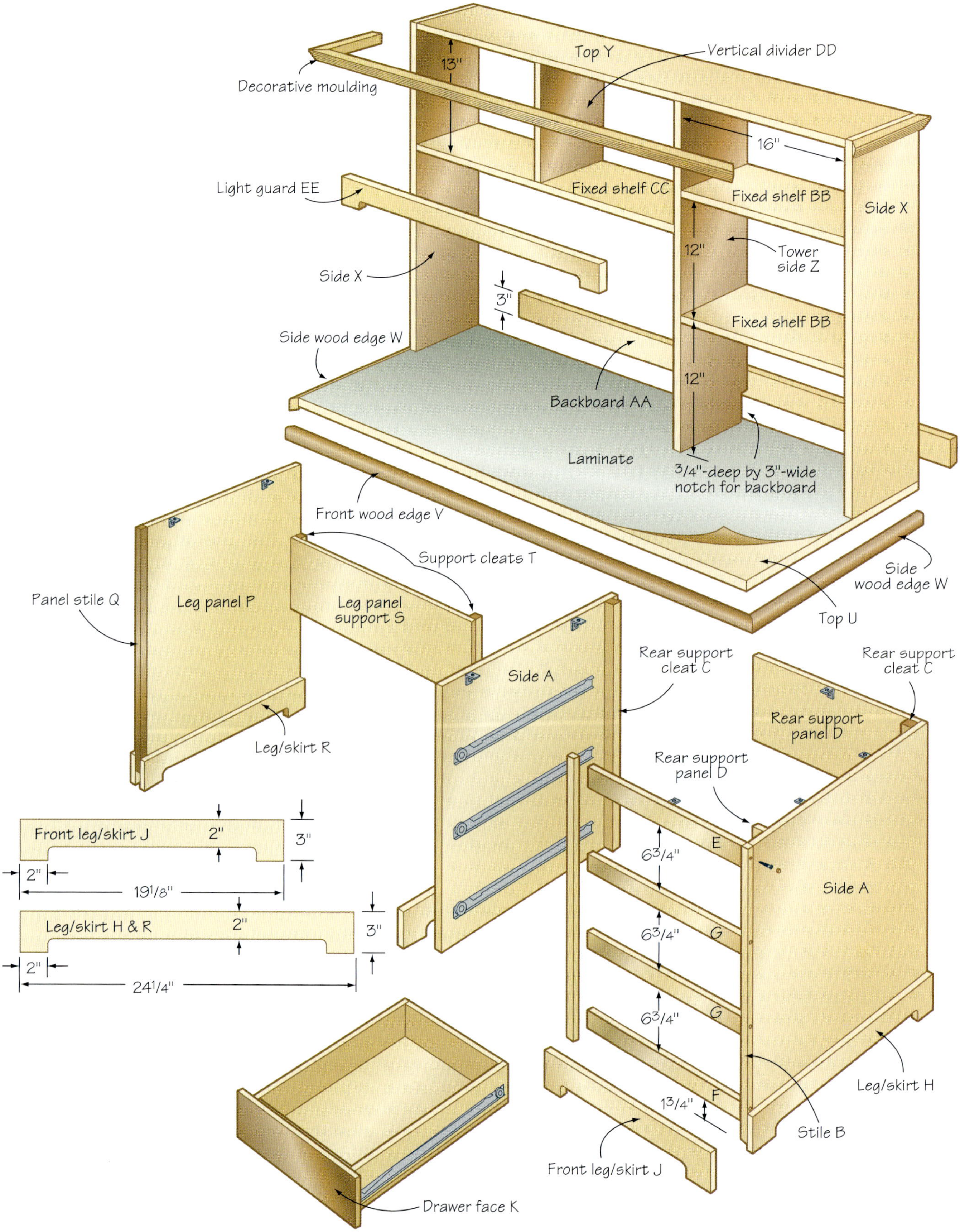
Top Y
Vertical divider DD
13"
Decorative moulding
16"
Light guard EE
Fixed shelf CC
Fixed shelf BB
Side X
12"
Tower side Z
Side X
3"
Fixed shelf BB
Side wood edge W
12"
Backboard AA
Laminate
3/4"-deep by 3"-wide notch for backboard
Front wood edge V
Support cleats T
Side wood edge W
Panel stile Q
Leg panel P
Leg panel support S
Top U
Side A
Rear support cleat C
Rear support cleat C
Rear support panel D
Leg/skirt R
Rear support panel D
Front leg/skirt J
2"
3"
E
6 3/4"
2"
19 1/8"
Side A
Leg/skirt H & R
2"
3"
6 3/4"
G
2"
24 1/4"
6 3/4"
G
Leg/skirt H
1 3/4"
F
Stile B
Front leg/skirt J
Drawer face K

INCHES (MILLIMETERS)

REFERENCE	QUANTITY	PART	STOCK	THICKNESS	(mm)	WIDTH	(mm)	LENGTH	(mm)
DRAWER BANK SECTION									
A	2	sides	veneer MDF	3/4	(19)	23 1/2	(597)	27 1/2	(699)
B	2	stiles	solid wood	3/4	(19)	3/4	(19)	29 1/4	(743)
C	2	rear support cleats	solid wood	3/4	(19)	3/4	(19)	27 1/2	(699)
D	2	rear support panels	veneer MDF	3/4	(19)	7	(178)	16	(406)
E	1	top rail	solid wood	3/4	(19)	2 1/4	(57)	16	(406)
F	1	bottom rail	solid wood	3/4	(19)	2	(51)	16	(406)
G	2	middle rails	solid wood	3/4	(19)	1 1/2	(38)	16	(406)
H	2	legs/skirts	solid wood	3/4	(19)	3	(76)	24 1/4	(616)
J	1	front leg/skirt	solid wood	3/4	(19)	3	(76)	19 1/8	(486)
K	3	drawer faces	solid wood	3/4	(19)	7 1/4	(184)	17	(432)
L	6	drawer sides	Baltic birch	1/2	(13)	5 1/4	(133)	22	(559)
M	6	drawer fronts & backs	Baltic birch	1/2	(13)	5 1/4	(133)	14	(356)
N	3	drawer bottoms	Baltic birch	1/2	(13)	15	(381)	22	(559)
LEG PANEL & SUPPORT									
P	1	leg panel	veneer MDF	3/4	(19)	23 1/2	(597)	27 1/2	(699)
Q	1	panel stile	solid wood	3/4	(19)	3/4	(19)	29 1/4	(743)
R	2	legs/skirts	solid wood	3/4	(19)	3/4	(19)	24 1/4	(616)
S	1	leg panel support	veneer MDF	3/4	(19)	7 1/4	(184)	29 3/4	(756)
T	2	support cleats	solid wood	3/4	(19)	3/4	(19)	7 1/4	(184)
DESKTOP									
U	1	top	particleboard	3/4	(19)	24 1/2	(622)	48	(1219)
V	1	front wood edge	solid wood	3/4	(19)	1 1/2	(38)	49 1/2	(1257)
W	2	side wood edges	solid wood	3/4	(19)	1 1/2	(38)	24 1/2	(622)
DESK HUTCH									
X	2	sides	solid wood	3/4	(19)	7 1/4	(184)	36	(914)
Y	1	top	solid wood	3/4	(19)	7 1/4	(184)	46 1/2	(1181)
Z	1	tower side	solid wood	3/4	(19)	7 1/4	(184)	35 1/4	(895)
AA	1	backboard	solid wood	3/4	(19)	3	(76)	46 1/2	(1181)
BB	2	fixed shelves	solid wood	3/4	(19)	7 1/4	(184)	16	(406)
CC	1	fixed shelf	solid wood	3/4	(19)	7 1/4	(184)	29 3/4	(756)
DD	1	vertical divider	solid wood	3/4	(19)	7 1/4	(184)	13	(330)
EE	1	light guard	solid wood	3/4	(19)	4	(102)	29 3/4	(756)

HARDWARE & SUPPLIES

3 sets–22" (559mm) bottom-mount drawer glides
3–drawer handles
6–right-angle brackets
1 piece–28" x 52" (711mm x 1321mm) high-pressure laminate
6' (2m) decorative moulding
2' (61cm) fluorescent light fixture
wood plugs
finishing and brad nails
wood filler
5/8" (16mm) PB screws
1" (25mm) PB screws
1 1/4" (32mm) PB screws
2" (51mm) PB screws
glue
colored putty
1 1/2" (38mm) screws
drawer pulls

Building the Drawer Bank and Leg Panel Assembly

1 Cut the two drawer bank sides A and the leg panel P, as they are all the same size. Each of the three panels requires a $\frac{3}{4}$" square stile B and Q, which are $29\frac{1}{4}$" long, applied to one face. Use glue and 2" finishing nails to secure the stiles. Attach each stile so it's flush with the top of the panel. That will make the stile extend $1\frac{3}{4}$" beyond the panel bottom. Countersink the nail heads and fill the holes with a colored putty to match the final finish.

2 Cut the two rear support cleats C and secure them to the inside face of each drawer bank side A with glue and $1\frac{1}{4}$" screws. The cleats are attached $\frac{3}{4}$" in from the back edge of each side. The two drawer bank sides should now be mirror images of each other. The stiles are on the front edges and the cleats on the inside back faces, forming a right and left side.

3 Attach the two rear support panels D with screws and glue as shown. These two pieces will not be visible, so any $\frac{3}{4}$"-thick material will be fine.

4 Install the drawer rails E, F and G as shown in the illustration. Use glue and 2" screws through the stiles B, in pilot holes that have been counter-bored to accept wood plugs.

5 The four side legs/skirt H and R, each $24\frac{1}{4}$" long, are now required. Cut the pattern as shown in the drawing. Use a $\frac{1}{4}$" roundover bit in a router to round the top, bottom and back edges on the outside face of each leg/skirt. If you don't own a router, ease the edges with sandpaper. Two will be attached to the drawer bank and two are for the side of the leg panel P. Attach the two legs/skirts H to the drawer bank and legs/skirts R to the leg panel. Use $1\frac{1}{4}$" screws and glue. The legs/skirts H and R are installed flush with the front face of stiles B and Q and $1\frac{1}{4}$" up from the bottom edge of the side A and leg panel P.

6 The front leg/skirt J is $19\frac{1}{8}$" long and cut as shown in the drawing. All edges of the face side should be rounded over. Attach the board using $1\frac{1}{4}$" screws and glue, aligning it to the side legs/skirts H. Three screws will hold the board securely until the adhesive cures. I cut it a little longer to provide a slight overhang on both sides so that the ends can be sanded flush to the side legs/skirts H after installation.

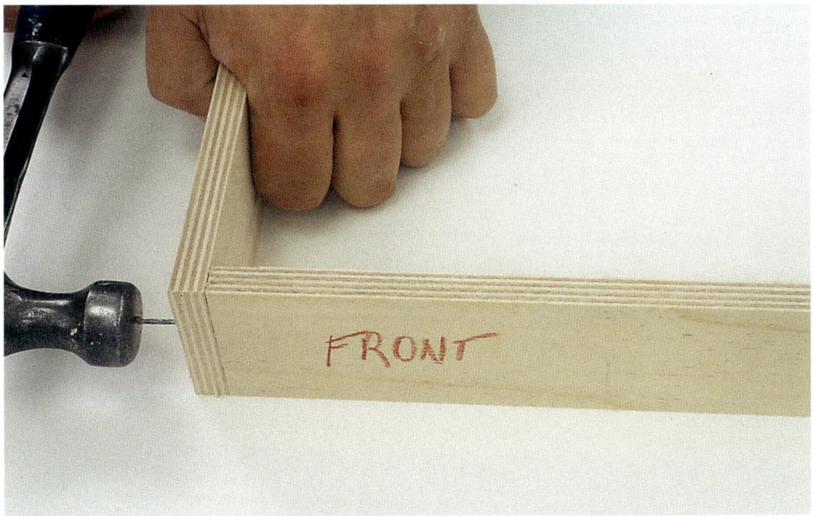

7 The bottom-mount drawer glides I used required a $\frac{1}{2}$" space per side for proper operation. Therefore, my drawer box is 1" narrower than the opening. Normally, my drawer box height is also 1" less. The drawer sides, back and front are made from Baltic birch plywood. The drawer bottom can be $\frac{1}{2}$" Baltic birch or $\frac{1}{4}$"-thick plywood; either is acceptable. Cut all the drawer box parts as detailed in the materials list and sand the edges smooth. Then join the sides L to the front and back M, using glue and finishing nails or $1\frac{1}{2}$"-long screws.

SHOP TIP

Cutting Patterns

When cutting multiple patterns such as the leg/skirt assemblies, create a pattern with scrap material to use as a guide. Then, after all the pieces are cut, clamp them together and sand the rough edges. This ensures that all the pieces are identical.

8 The drawer bottom N is attached using glue and finishing nails. The bottom should be cut square and aligned to all faces of the drawer box. If it is square and aligned, your drawer box will be square.

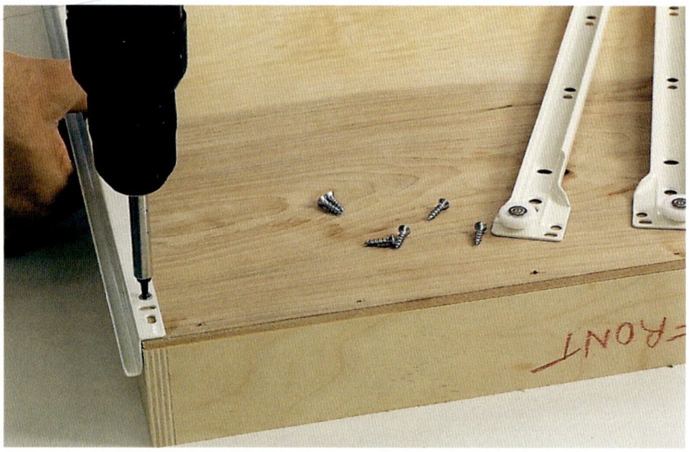

9 Install the 22" bottom-mount drawer glides by first attaching the runners to the drawer box.

10 Use a carpenter's square to draw a line $\frac{3}{4}$" up from each rail to make a screw hole line for the two cabinet runners of each drawer glide set.

11 Make the three drawer faces K using 1x8 lumber. Trim to the size indicated and round over all edges of the outside face with a $\frac{1}{4}$" router bit. Attach the drawer faces with 1" screws through the drawer box. Each face should overlap its top and bottom rail by $\frac{1}{4}$".

12 To complete the drawer bank, install right-angle brackets around the top edge. These will be used to secure the desktop.

SHOP TIP

Mounting Drawer Fronts

Mounting drawer fronts accurately can be difficult. But here is an easy method. First, drill the handle holes in the drawer face only. Then, hold the drawer face in position and drive screws through the handle holes into the drawer box. Remove the drawer with the face attached and secure the face from the rear. Finally, remove the screws, complete drilling the holes through the drawer box, and install your handle hardware. You'll have perfectly aligned faces every time!

Constructing the Hutch

13 Begin building the desk hutch by joining the two sides X to the top Y. Use glue and 2" wood screws. The screw heads will be covered by trim moulding, so they can be driven flush with the side surfaces.

14 Cut the tower side Z to the dimensions shown in the materials list. Before installing, notch the bottom back edge for the backboard AA. Secure the tower side Z to the top Y, using 2" wood screws in piloted counterbored holes that can be filled with wood plugs. Install the tower side Z leaving a 16" space for the fixed shelves BB.

15 Backboard AA is installed to strengthen the hutch and is attached to the sides X and tower side Z with screws and glue. Fill the holes on the outside faces of the sides X with wood plugs.

16 Attach the fixed shelves BB and CC, and vertical divider DD with glue and 2" wood screws. Fill the holes with plugs. Shelf spacing and the number of fixed shelves required depend on your storage needs. Customize this section to suit your requirements.

17 If you plan to install a 2' fluorescent lamp under the long shelf, the optional light guard EE, cut in the same style as the legs/skirt, will conceal the fixture. It's attached with glue and screws through the sides X and Z, as well as the top of the long fixed shelf CC.

18 Erase all the front edges of the hutch with a ¼" roundover bit in a router, with the exception of the top Y. If you plan to install 1"-high decorative moulding as I've done, stop the roundover procedure at a point where the moulding crosses the hutch's vertical boards. This will provide a square flat surface to attach the decorative moulding.

19 Choose a suitable decorative moulding for the top of the hutch. Secure it with glue and brad nails. You'll need about 6' of moulding and a miter box to cut the 45° corners.

BUILDING THE DESKTOP

The desktop for this project is made with a 3/4"-thick particleboard or plywood substrate. Wood edges are attached to the front and two sides of the substrate. Then a high-pressure laminate is glued to the substrate, using contact cement. Finally, the laminate is trimmed and rounded over with a router bit. Follow the procedures detailed in project one of chapter two to make your wood-edged laminate desktop.

You'll need a 3/4" top U 24 1/2" deep by 48" long. The front wood edge V is a 3/4"-thick by 1 1/2"-high solid piece of wood 49 1/2" long. The two side wood edges W are the same height and thickness and are 24 1/2" long.

The laminate material should be about 28" × 52". It's larger than the top, but you'll need a little extra material because it's difficult to align. The overhang can be cut with a flush-trim router bit. High-pressure laminates are an excellent choice for this desktop as they provide a smooth writing surface that will handle a great deal of abuse.

ASSEMBLING THE WORK CENTER

From this point forward, all the assembly will be done using screws. Glue should not be used in case the desk needs to be taken apart for moving or you need to replace the desktop due to wear or damage.

Attach the leg panel assembly to the drawer bank case using leg panel support S. The leg panel support S is held in place by the two support cleats T — one on the leg panel P and the other attached to the drawer bank side. Secure it with 1 1/4" wood screws about midpoint on each assembly. Then, install two right-angle brackets on leg panel P so it can be attached to the underside of the desktop. Set the desktop on the drawer bank and leg panel. Secure the top to the drawer bank and leg panel with 5/8"-long screws in the right-angle brackets.

Place the hutch on top of the desk. Align the backboard AA with the back edge of the desktop. Install two 2" wood screws from the underside of the desktop into the backboard AA to secure it in place. Install the drawers and verify all the components fit and operate properly. Once the test fitting is complete, take the assemblies apart and apply a finish.

CHAPTER four

Improving Kitchen Storage

Many kitchens have a storage problem. There's never enough space for all the canned goods, packaged foods, flour, sugar and other bulk purchases. We cram all these goods in every corner of our kitchens, then finding them is sometimes quite a challenge.

Here's a project that just might solve your kitchen storage problem. It measures 3' wide by 2' deep, but this small cabinet can easily store two weeks of groceries.

I've made this cabinet with pine veneer medium-density fiberboard (MDF). The raised-panel stile-and-rail doors are made of solid pine. They can be purchased or built in your workshop.

The heart of this pantry is the pullout shelf system. I've used an adjustable version manufactured by Knape & Vogt Manufacturing Company, but you can make your own pullouts using standard drawer glides. If you want a simple and inexpensive version, install adjustable shelves.

A freestanding dry goods pantry doesn't have to be located in a kitchen. It can be installed in the basement to store preserves or in a room close by the kitchen if the space is limited. And finally, you don't have to use this pantry for food; this project has dozens of other useful applications.

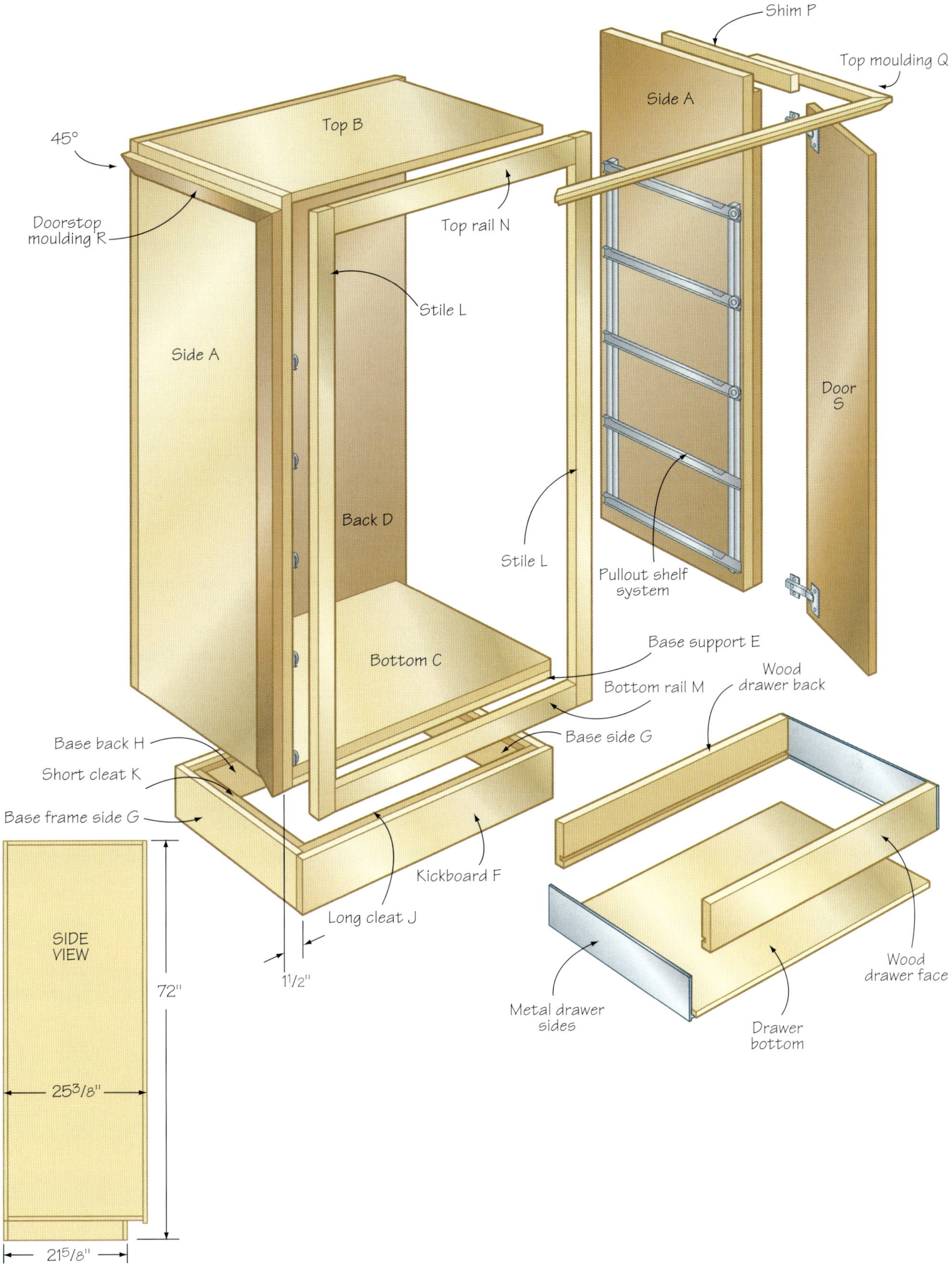
Shim P
Top moulding Q
Side A
Top B
45°
Doorstop
moulding R
Top rail N
Stile L
Side A
Door
S
Back D
Stile L
Pullout shelf
system
Bottom C
Base support E
Wood
drawer back
Bottom rail M
Base side G
Base back H
Short cleat K
Base frame side G
Kickboard F
Long cleat J
1 1/2"
Metal drawer
sides
Wood
drawer face
Drawer
bottom
SIDE
VIEW
72"
25 3/8"
21 5/8"

INCHES (MILLIMETERS)

REFERENCE	QUANTITY	PART	STOCK	THICKNESS	(mm)	WIDTH	(mm)	LENGTH	(mm)
A	2	sides	veneer MDF	3/4	(19)	23 7/8	(606)	68	(1727)
B	1	top	veneer MDF	3/4	(19)	23 7/8	(606)	34 1/2	(876)
C	1	bottom	veneer MDF	3/4	(19)	23 7/8	(606)	34 1/2	(876)
D	1	back	veneer MDF	3/4	(19)	36	(914)	68	(1727)
E	1	base support	plywood	1/2	(13)	24 5/8	(625)	36	(914)
F	1	kickboard	solid wood	3/4	(19)	3 1/2	(89)	33	(838)
G	2	base sides	solid wood	3/4	(19)	3 1/2	(89)	20 3/8	(518)
H	1	base back	solid wood	3/4	(19)	3 1/2	(89)	31 1/2	(800)
J	2	long cleats	solid wood	3/4	(19)	3/4	(19)	31 1/2	(800)
K	2	short cleats	solid wood	3/4	(19)	3/4	(19)	18	(457)
L	2	stiles	solid wood	3/4	(19)	1	(25)	68 1/2	(1740)
M	1	bottom rail	solid wood	3/4	(19)	1 1/4	(32)	34 1/2	(876)
N	1	top rail	solid wood	3/4	(19)	1 1/2	(38)	34 1/2	(876)
P	2	shims	solid wood	1/4	(6)	1 1/8	(29)	24 5/8	(625)
Q		top moulding	solid wood					8'	(2.5m)
R		doorstop moulding	solid wood					40'	(12m)
S	2	doors	wood	3/4	(19)	17 3/4	(451)	67 1/4	(1708)

HARDWARE & SUPPLIES

material for pullouts or fixed shelves as required
3/8" (10mm) wood plugs
glue
2" (51mm) finish nails and 1"
(25mm) brads
1" (25mm) PB screws
1 1/2" (38mm) PB screws
2" (51mm) PB screws
wood filler
6 hidden hinges and plates
2 door pulls
colored wood putty

1 Cut the two cabinet sides A, top B and bottom C as detailed in the materials list. Join the sides to the top and bottom, using glue and 2" screws that are designed for particleboard (PB). For maximum hold, remember to predrill prior to installing the screws. The cabinet box should measure 36" wide by 68" high.

2 Attach the back D with glue and 2" PB screws in predrilled holes. An accurately cut back will square the cabinet box.

3 This cabinet will carry a great deal of weight so I want to reinforce the bottom C. Use a piece of $\frac{1}{2}$"-thick plywood for the base support E. Glue and screw it in place using 1" screws.

4 Mark a line on the bottom of the base support $3\frac{1}{2}$" in from the cabinet front and $1\frac{1}{2}$" in from each side to indicate the base frame position. Construct a base frame $3\frac{1}{2}$" high using parts F, G and H. The frame dimension will be $21\frac{5}{8}$" deep by 33" wide. Assemble the frame with glue and 2" screws in counterbored holes, and fill the holes with wood plugs.

5 Cut the four cleats J and K as detailed in the materials list. Glue and screw them to the inside top edge of the base frame. Apply glue to the top edge of the base frame and place the assembly on the base using the guide marks. Screw through the cleats into the base with $1\frac{1}{2}$" screws.

6 The stiles L (vertical members) of the face frame are installed first. Their width is dependent on the side moulding thickness. I am using pine doorstop moulding that is $\frac{1}{4}$" thick, so my stile width is the side A thickness plus the moulding, or 1". Each stile is $68\frac{1}{2}$" high and should be installed flush with the top and bottom of the cabinet. Use glue and 2" finish nails to nail the stiles L to each cabinet side edge. Be sure the inside edge of stile L is flush with the inside face of side A. Set the nail heads and fill the holes with colored wood putty.

7 The bottom rail M is attached in the same manner as the stiles were. Its bottom edge should be aligned to the ends of each stile L.

8 Attach the top rail N. Its top edge should be flush with the ends of each stile L.

9 Glue and nail both shims P to both top edges of the cabinet. These strips will allow easy installation of the trim moulding.

10 Choose a top moulding Q to suit your décor. I am using $1\frac{1}{8}$"-high moulding, but any size or style is fine. If the moulding is higher than $1\frac{1}{8}$", install it above the cabinet top. Do not attach moulding lower than $1\frac{1}{8}$" below the top edge as we will need door opening clearance.

11 Once the top moulding Q is attached, install the doorstop moulding R around the perimeter of each side. Use glue and brad nails. Miter each corner with the round edge of the moulding facing inward.

12 This cabinet has many shelving options. Adjustable shelves work well for this application, or you also have the option to use standard drawer glides for pullout shelves. I'm using a system of adjustable pull-outs that can be purchased at kitchen hardware supply stores.

13 The system that I used comes with metal slides, metal drawer sides and support assemblies. All that's left to make are the drawer faces, backs and bottoms. The wood for the faces normally matches the cabinet wood.

Door Options

Any number of door styles can be used on the pantry cabinet. You'll need two doors, each 17¾" wide by 67¼" high. I would suggest that you use three full-overlay hidden hinges per door because of their size. Using these types of hinges makes door width calculations easier.

I prefer to cover the bottom rail with a door and overlap the top rail by ¼". The distance from the bottom rail to the inside edge of the top rail is 67". Add ¼" for overlap and the door height will be 67¼". That's a standard method for calculating door heights for cabinets with full-overlay doors.

The width of any cabinet door or pair of doors is also easily calculated. Measure the inside opening of the cabinet. In this case, it's 34½". If you have stiles extending into the cabinet, measure their inside dimension. In this case, however, the inside edges of the stiles are mounted flush with the interior face of the cabinet sides.

Add 1" to that dimension for a total measurement of 35½". Therefore, the cabinet requires two 17¾"-wide doors that are 67¼" high.

Flat- or raised-panel doors can be made with a table saw; you don't need router bits to make one or two doors. See the following "Shop Talk" if you wish to make your own doors.

shop talk | *Making Table Saw Frame Doors*

Build two doors 17¾" wide by 67¼" high with a center rail.

INCHES (MILLIMETERS)

REFERENCE	QUANTITY	PART	STOCK	THICKNESS	(mm)	WIDTH	(mm)	LENGTH	(mm)	COMMENTS
A	4	stiles		¾	(19)	2¼	(57)	67½	(1715)	
B	6	rails		¾	(19)	2¼	(57)	14¾	(375)	includes ¼" x ¾" (6mm x 19mm) tenon on each end
C	4	center panels		¼	(6)	14¾	(375)	31¾	(806)	

1 Cut the stiles and rails to the sizes required. Use a table saw to form a ¼"-wide by ¾"-deep groove along one edge of each piece. To ensure the groove is centered on your ¾" stock, set the inside face of the saw blade ¼" away from the fence. Push each board through the blade, then reverse the board and run it through the blade again. That process will center the groove but may leave a small strip of material in the middle if your blade is less than ⅛" thick. If that's the case, adjust the fence and run a cleaning pass in the center of each groove.

2 Each of the four rails requires a ¼"-thick by ¾"-long tenon centered on both ends. These can be cut with a standard saw blade by making multiple passes over the blade or with a dado blade. Test the cuts on scrap material to be sure the tenons fit properly in the grooves.

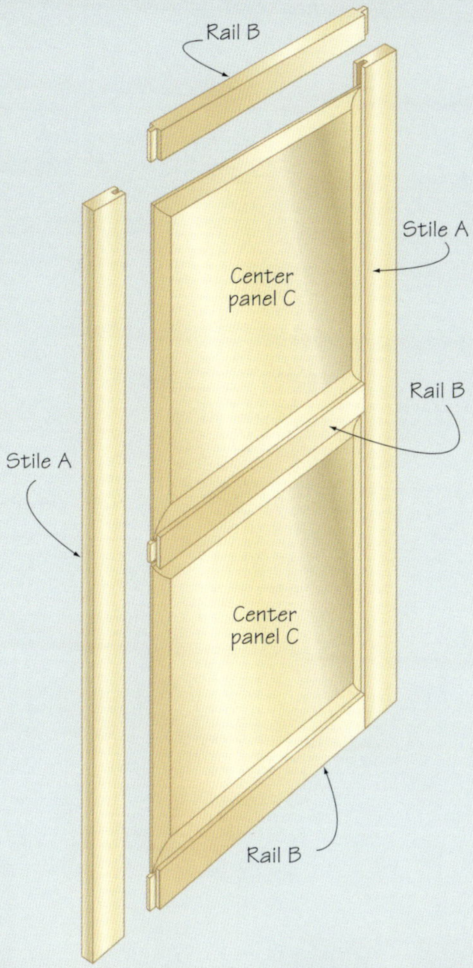

3 At this point, the center panels can be flat or raised. To make flat-panel doors, use ¼"-thick veneer plywood cut to the size indicated in the materials list, then proceed to step 5 to assemble the doors.

Or you can make a raised center panel with solid ¾"-thick stock on a table saw. First, however, you must edge-glue boards to form a panel. Refer to "Making Solid Wood Panel Glue-Ups" in chapter one and cut them to the size indicated above. To raise solid panels on a table saw, lower the blade below the table surface and secure a strong board across its center at 90° to the blade face. The best blade for this technique is a large-kerf (thick) rip blade. The miter slide can be used to align the guide board.

4 Begin with the blade ⅓₂" above the table surface. Push all four sides of each center panel across the blade. Repeat the process, raising the blade ⅓₂" after each series of passes, until the edges of the panels fit loosely into the stile and rail grooves. Be sure the panels move freely inside the grooves to allow for expansion and contraction of the wood. Slow, steady passes across the blade will yield the best cuts and reduce the amount of sanding needed after the cuts have been completed. Use a push pad in the center of each panel so it won't tip as the edges get thinner.

5 Sand the panel edges and assemble the doors, using glue on the tenons only. Clamp them securely until the glue sets up. The center panels should float in the grooves. Ensure the frames are square by measuring the diagonals. If the dimensions are the same, the panel is square. Tall doors, such as the ones required for the pantry project, need a center rail to strengthen the door. It's located at the center point of the stiles and requires a tenon on each end as well as a groove on both edges to receive the upper and lower panels.

simple storage wardrobe | *page 78*

low-cost storage shelving | *page 85*

Basement/Garage Storage Ideas

closet storage | *page 89*

Those of us who live in colder areas, where ground frost is an issue, have basements under our homes. They add extra living space when properly finished and house all those necessary mechanical systems needed for the cold.

Basements also provide extra storage space for seasonal items such as clothes, ski equipment, summer furniture and winter snow-handling equipment. Often, basements are not well organized, so here are three projects that may help in the never-ending battle to keep the basement neat.

The wardrobe project can be used in the basement but is also handy for clothes storage in any room. The second project is a storage rack with an adjustable shelf feature. You don't need to spend a lot of money for lumber here; any construction-grade 2×4s and some $^3/_4$" particleboard or plywood for shelving is all you'll need to make this handy shelf unit.

PROJECT 1

simple storage wardrobe

The wardrobe project in this section is simple to build and may just be the answer to your storage problem. This one was constructed with oak veneer sheet material, but it could be just as easily built with plain MDF or particleboard and painted. I've made mine a little fancier than normal by using solid oak corner and crown moulding. But again, it isn't necessary to spend the extra money if you're looking only for a plain and simple wardrobe. Commercially made wardrobes are somewhat expensive. And if they have a drawer like the one in this project, the price really climbs.

You should save a considerable sum of money by building your own wardrobe. The final cost, however, is dependent on what type of sheet material you decide to use, the size of the wardrobe and the cost of solid-wood trim that might be added.

You can trim out the cabinet using iron-on veneer edge tape, which is easier and much less costly. The only other change would be how the back is installed and the bottom and top boards are joined to the sides. If you have the equipment, use biscuits to join the sides to both bottom and top boards. The back should be set into rabbet cuts on panels A and B and shelf K will have to be reduced in depth by $\frac{1}{4}$", or the depth of the rabbet cuts, for the back. This alternative building method would be simpler and one that I will consider for my next wardrobe, but the choice is yours.

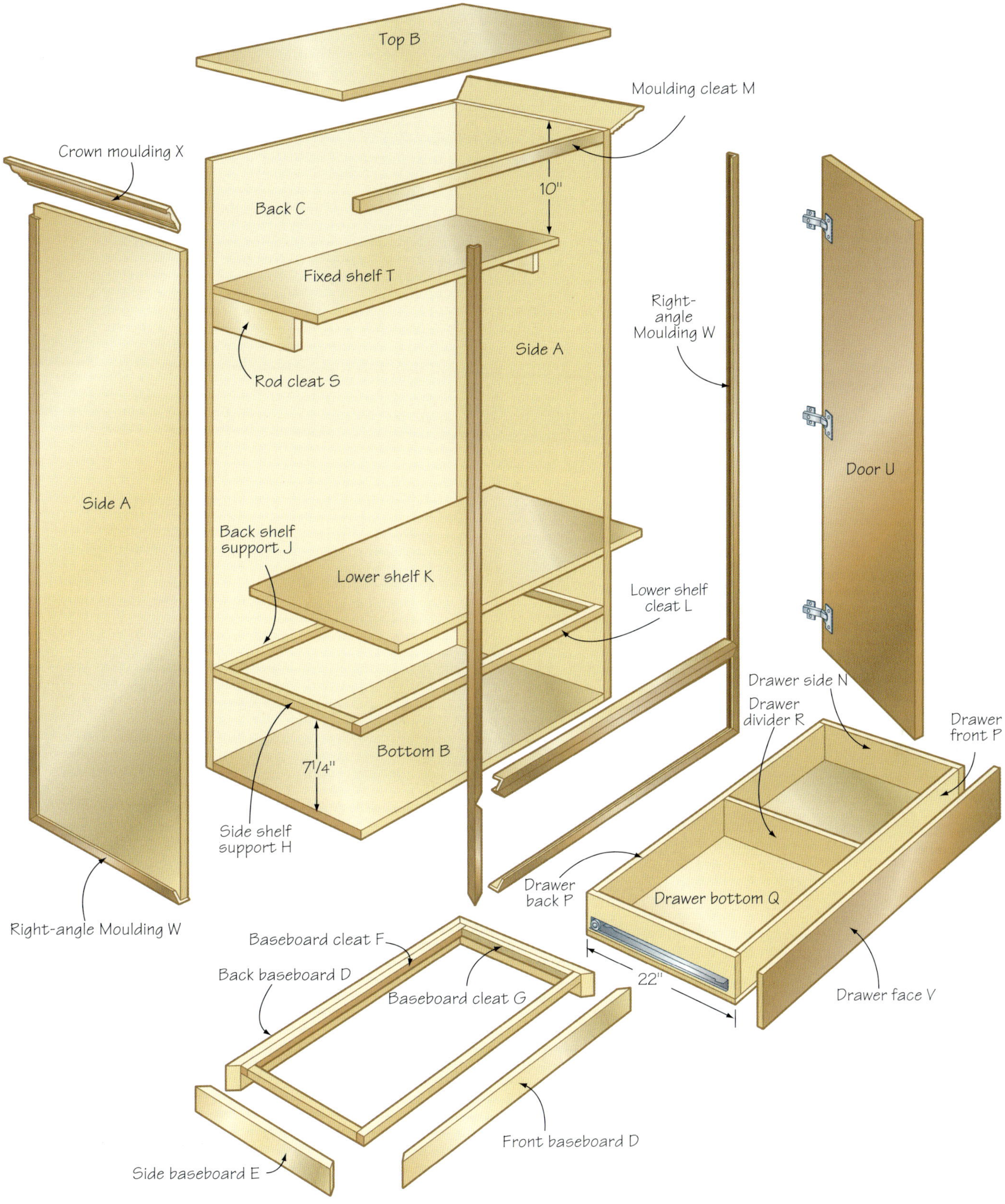
Top B
Moulding cleat M
Crown moulding X
10"
Back C
Fixed shelf T
Right-
angle
Moulding W
Side A
Rod cleat S
Door U
Side A
Back shelf
support J
Lower shelf K
Lower shelf
cleat L
Drawer side N
Drawer
divider R
Drawer
front P
Bottom B
7 1/4"
Side shelf
support H
Drawer
back P
Drawer bottom Q
Right-angle Moulding W
Baseboard cleat F
Back baseboard D
Baseboard cleat G
22"
Drawer face V
Front baseboard D
Side baseboard E

INCHES (MILLIMETERS)

REFERENCE	QUANTITY	PART	STOCK	THICKNESS	(mm)	WIDTH	(mm)	LENGTH	(mm)
A	2	sides	veneer PB	$^{11}/_{16}$	(18)	$23^{1}/_{2}$	(597)	80	(2032)
B	2	top & bottom	veneer PB	$^{11}/_{16}$	(18)	$23^{1}/_{2}$	(597)	$46^{5}/_{8}$	(1184)
C	1	back	veneer ply	$^{1}/_{4}$	(6)	48	(1219)	80	(2032)
D	2	front & back baseboards	veneer PB	$^{11}/_{16}$	(18)	3	(76)	44	(1118)
E	2	side baseboards	veneer PB	$^{11}/_{16}$	(18)	3	(76)	$19^{3}/_{4}$	(502)
F	2	baseboard cleats	hardwood	$^{3}/_{4}$	(19)	$^{3}/_{4}$	(19)	42	(1067)
G	2	baseboard cleats	hardwood	$^{3}/_{4}$	(19)	$^{3}/_{4}$	(19)	17	(432)
H	2	side shelf supports	hardwood	$^{3}/_{4}$	(19)	$^{3}/_{4}$	(19)	$22^{3}/_{4}$	(578)
J	1	back shelf support	hardwood	$^{3}/_{4}$	(19)	$^{3}/_{4}$	(19)	$45^{1}/_{8}$	(1146)
K	1	lower shelf	veneer PB	$^{11}/_{16}$	(18)	$23^{1}/_{2}$	(597)	$46^{5}/_{8}$	(1184)
L	1	lower shelf cleat	veneer PB	$^{11}/_{16}$	(18)	$^{3}/_{4}$	(19)	$46^{5}/_{8}$	(1184)
M	1	moulding cleat	veneer PB	$^{11}/_{16}$	(18)	$^{3}/_{4}$	(19)	$46^{5}/_{8}$	(1184)
N	2	drawer sides	Baltic birch	$^{1}/_{2}$	(13)	$5^{1}/_{2}$	(140)	22	(559)
P	2	drawer front & back	Baltic birch	$^{1}/_{2}$	(13)	$5^{1}/_{2}$	(140)	$44^{5}/_{8}$	(1134)
Q	1	drawer bottom	Baltic birch	$^{1}/_{2}$	(13)	22	(559)	$45^{5}/_{8}$	(1159)
R	1	drawer divider	Baltic birch	$^{1}/_{2}$	(13)	$5^{1}/_{2}$	(140)	21	(533)
S	2	rod cleats	hardwood	$^{3}/_{4}$	(19)	$3^{1}/_{2}$	(89)	14	(356)
T	1	fixed shelf	veneer PB	$^{11}/_{16}$	(18)	16	(406)	$46^{5}/_{8}$	(1184)
U	2	doors	veneer PB	$^{11}/_{16}$	(18)	$23^{13}/_{16}$	(605)	70	(1778)
V	1	drawer face	veneer PB	$^{11}/_{16}$	(18)	$8^{1}/_{2}$	(216)	$47^{3}/_{4}$	(1213)
W		right angle moulding		$^{11}/_{16}$	(18)	$^{11}/_{16}$	(18)	48'	(14.6m)
X		crown moulding				$3^{1}/_{8}$	(79)	8'	(2.4m)

HARDWARE & SUPPLIES

6–107° European hidden hinges
3–handles
1 set–22" (559mm) bottom mount drawer glide
1 clothes rod or $1^{1}/_{2}$" (38mm)
diameter wood dowel
glue
brad nails
2" (51mm) PB screws
finishing nails
$1^{1}/_{4}$" (32mm) PB screws
1" (25mm) PB screws
wood buttons
iron-on edge tape

Building the Storage Wardrobe

1 Cut the two sides A, as well as the top and bottom B to the sizes detailed in the materials list. Attach the sides to the top and bottom. They should be flush with the ends of each side board. Use glue and five 2" PB screws per joint. Install the screws through the side panels, but be sure to drill pilot holes for the particleboard screws to insure maximum hold.

2 Install the $^{1}/_{4}$" thick veneer plywood back C. Glue and finishing nails, spaced about 8" apart, will hold the panel securely.

3 While the case is lying flat, build a base according to the dimensions given in the materials list, using parts D, E, F and G. The base is made from $^{11}/_{16}$"-thick veneer particleboard cut at 45° to form the corners. The $^{3}/_{4}$" square hardwood cleats F and G are attached to the base frame with glue and $1^{1}/_{4}$" screws. These cleats are used to attach the base to the case with glue and screws. The base frame is mounted 2" in from all edges. Apply glue to the base and, using $1^{1}/_{4}$" long particleboard screws, attach it to the bottom of the wardrobe case.

SHOP TIP

Be extra careful when cutting any cabinet back. If it's cut squarely, it will square the cabinet you are building. You can verify that your cabinet is square by making sure the diagonal measurements are equal.

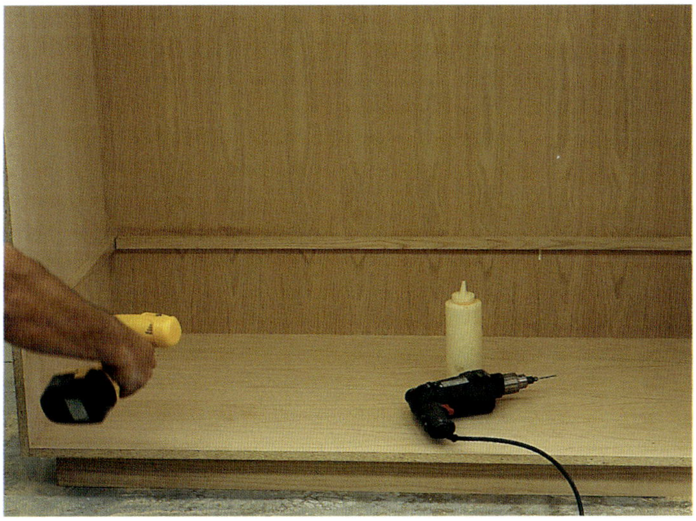

4 Cut the side and back shelf supports H and J. The side supports H are attached to the case sides A with $1^{1}/_{4}$" screws and glue from the interior of the wardrobe. The bottom edges of H and J are $7^{1}/_{4}$" above the top surface of the bottom B. The back support J is held in place by 1" screws through the back of the back C and into the support. Note that the side supports H are set back $^{3}/_{4}$" from the front edges of sides A.

5 Cut the lower shelf K, but before installing the shelf on the shelf supports, attach the lower shelf cleat L to the underside of the front edge. Use glue and brad nails to secure the cleat. The $^{11}/_{16}$" dimension of the cleat should be vertical. To verify that you have installed it correctly, the bottom shelf front thickness should be $1^{3}/_{8}$".

6 Apply glue to the top of all shelf supports H and J and install the shelf K. It is secured in place with a few finishing nails through the top face and into the supports.

7 Moulding cleat M should be installed on the underside of the top B at this time. Follow the same procedures as detailed in step 5.

8 If you decided to use iron-on veneer edge tape, you can skip this step. The edge trim is right-angle hardwood moulding W. It measures $^{11}/_{16}$" x $^{11}/_{16}$" on the inside faces. This moulding is a standard item and available in most wood supply stores. The moulding is cut at 45° at all corners. However, on the lower shelf K and fixed shelf T, the horizontal moulding strips must be trimmed square after the 45° is cut. A straight cut, where the moulding sides meet at the back of the 45°, is needed so it will properly join the vertical moulding strips. Use a miter box to accurately cut the moulding. Apply corner moulding to the front closet section, as well as the drawer section. Carefully miter the corners. The top and shelf trim is installed on the inside of the cabinet while the bottom trim is on the outside. Glue and nail the mouldings to each side. You'll need one strip on the bottom and one on each front and back edge. Stop the moulding $^{11}/_{16}$" from the top to allow room for attaching the crown. The 45° cuts that meet at the outside intersection of the bottom shelf will create a wedge gap. This can be filled by cutting a small wedge and carefully pushing it into the hole. Glue is all that's needed to hold the wedge in place.

9 I've used $3^{1}/_{8}$"-high crown moulding X for the top of my wardrobe. Cut the moulding upside down in your miter box to achieve the correct 45° angle. The crown is attached with glue and finishing nails. It should be installed $^{11}/_{16}$" down from the top of each side A.

Building the Drawer Box

10 This drawer box, like a few other projects in this book, is made with $\frac{1}{2}$"-thick Baltic birch plywood. Refer to project three in chapter three for details on building this type of drawer box. The corner joints can be butt joined with glue and screws, or the front and back P can be set in $\frac{1}{4}$"-deep by $\frac{1}{2}$"-wide rabbets in the sides N and secured with glue and brad nails. My drawer calls for a butt joint at each corner, but you can cut a rabbet in the sides and increase the length of each front and back P by $\frac{1}{2}$". However, remember the rule when installing drawer glides. Most manufacturers require $\frac{1}{2}$" clearance per side. It's also good practice to build the drawer box at least 1" less than the available vertical space. I've used 22" bottom-mount drawer glides and added a center divider R in the box for added strength. Baltic birch — or as it's sometimes called, cabinet-grade plywood — is void free. Therefore, the exposed edges can be sanded smooth.

Attaching Hanging Hardware

11 Mount the two rod cleats S, 10" down from the top B. Drill pilot holes and attach the cleats with glue and $1\frac{1}{4}$" screws. Plug the screw head holes with wood buttons.

12 The fixed shelf T is $\frac{11}{16}$" thick by 16" deep and $46\frac{5}{8}$" wide. Apply glue on top of the rod cleats S and secure the shelf T with a few brad nails. This shelf should have its front edge covered with iron-on edge tape. Mount a clothes rod about 12" out from the back. I've used a commercial version that was made from metal.

Making the Doors and Drawer Face

The two doors U and one drawer face V can be cut from one sheet of material. Before ripping the door widths, crosscut the drawer face. Calculating door widths when using European hidden hinges is simple. First, measure the inside cabinet, then, add 1" to that dimension and divide by two. That will be the door width.

My doors U and drawer front V are made from $^{11}/_{16}$"-thick veneer particleboard.

Cut the two doors and one drawer face. Apply edge tape to all exposed edges before installing.

To install the doors, use three 107° European hidden hinges for each door. The bottom edge of the drawer face V is flush with the lower edge of bottom B. It's attached with four 1"-long screws through the drawer box. Leave a $^{1}/_{2}$" gap between the top edge of the drawer face and bottom edge of the doors.

Construction Options

Dozens of door options are available. However, frame-and-panel models made by a door factory will be expensive because these are large doors. You can build your own frame-and-panel doors as shown in chapter two or the style shown in chapter four. Veneer particleboard doors with taped edges are reasonably priced but very plain looking. If you want something a little fancier without spending a great deal of money, you can add moulding to the door slab.

The corner trim is an option you can eliminate. It's a different treatment and one that requires a fair amount of patience. Simply applying wood veneer edge tape to all exposed edges is an acceptable and less costly alternative, as mentioned at the start of this project.

A 1$^{1}/_{2}$"-diameter wood dowel can be used for the hanging rod. But the commercial metal version is adjustable and easy to install. A wide variety of accessories are available for closets nowadays as well, so it would be worth your time to browse through the home store for additional ideas.

Less-expensive sheet goods can be used if you plan to paint the wardrobe. If, for example, you need a clothing storage center in your basement, use $^{3}/_{4}$" particleboard or MDF. Give the wardrobe a couple of coats of good paint and you'll have a great storage center for all those seasonal clothes.

And finally, the wardrobe can be any size you need to fit your requirements or space allowance. I've got a lot of room available, so mine is 48" wide. However, this project can just as easily be constructed to any size that suits your needs.

PROJECT 2

low-cost storage shelving

It seems that I'm always looking for extra shelf space in the basement or workshop. Simply sticking together a few boards isn't always suitable because storage needs are always changing. I wanted a low-cost, adjustable shelf that could be moved if necessary.

A materials list did not seem appropriate for this project, as everyone's storage space is unique. So determine your requirements and adjust the dimensions accordingly.

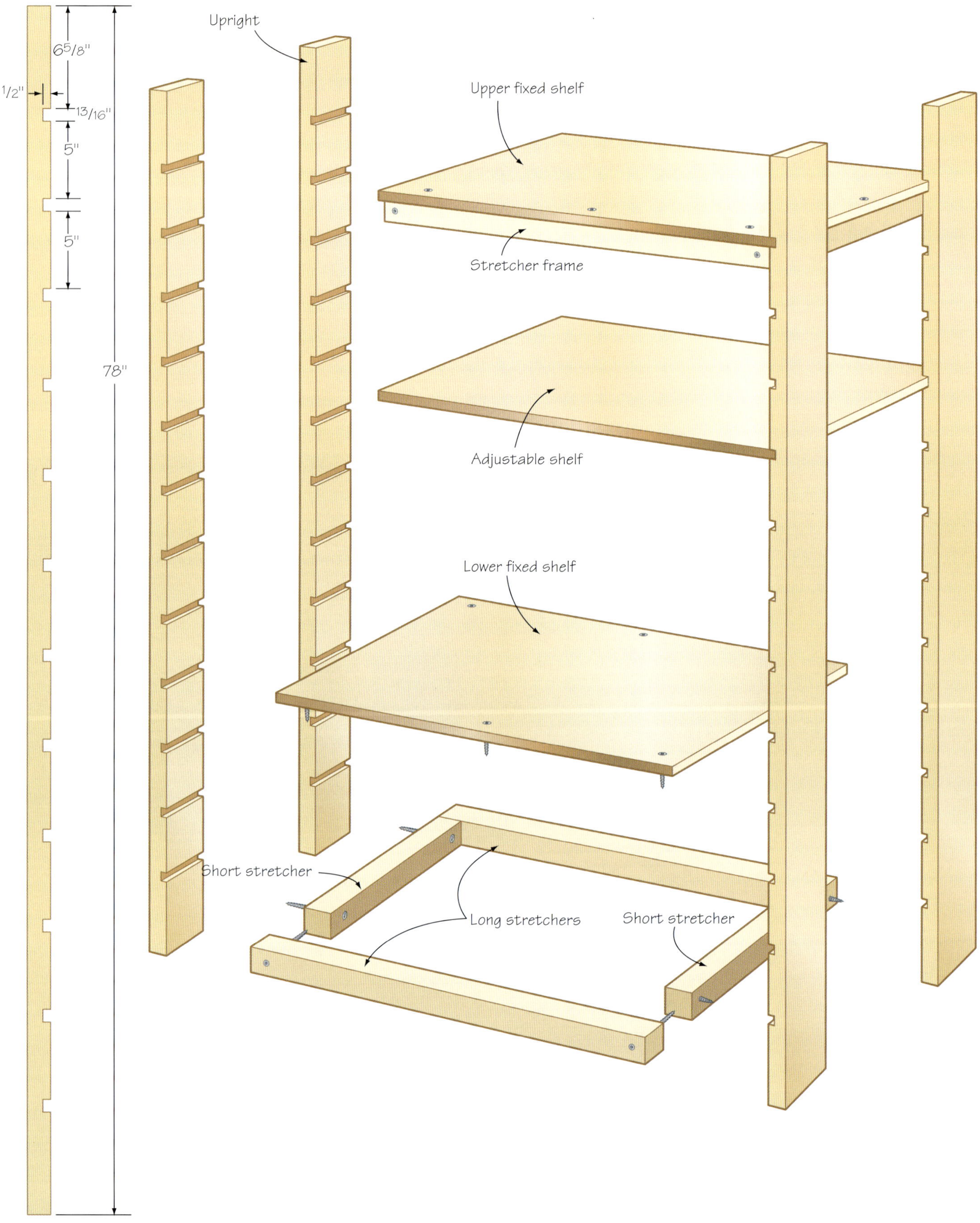
6 5/8"
1/2"
13/16"
5"
5"
78"
Upright
Upper fixed shelf
Stretcher frame
Adjustable shelf
Lower fixed shelf
Short stretcher
Long stretchers
Short stretcher

1 Measure the maximum height allowed in the area where you plan to keep the shelf unit. In my case, I had about 78" of free space in the basement storage room. For each shelf unit I cut four uprights at 1½" x 3½" x 78" long. I made one unit with pressure-treated pine and the other with red cedar. Use a radial-arm or table saw with a dado blade and cut dadoes for the adjustable shelf system on the inside face of each upright to the dimensions detailed in the drawing.

2 For each shelf unit, cut four boards at 1½" x 1½" x 8½" long and four at 1½" x 1½" x 30" long. Join two short and two long pieces, with glue and 3" screws in pilot holes, to form a stretcher that measures 11½" deep and 30" long. Use the remaining four boards to make a second stretcher.

SHOP TIP

I plan to use particleboard shelves that are ¾" thick by 11½" deep by 31" wide. These sizes maximize the cutting yield from a sheet of 4' x 8' material. I suggest you do not exceed a shelf width of 32" unless you plan to add support braces. Heavy loads on a shelf that has a large span can bend or break the shelf board.

3 Attach the stretchers to four uprights, using 2" wood screws. One stretcher assembly is secured directly below the top dadoes in each upright, and the other is directly below the bottom dadoes.

4 Cut two fixed shelves at $\frac{3}{4}$" x $11\frac{1}{2}$" x 31" wide. Install one directly above the top stretcher and the other above the bottom stretcher in their respective dadoes. Secure the shelves to the stretchers with 2" wood screws.

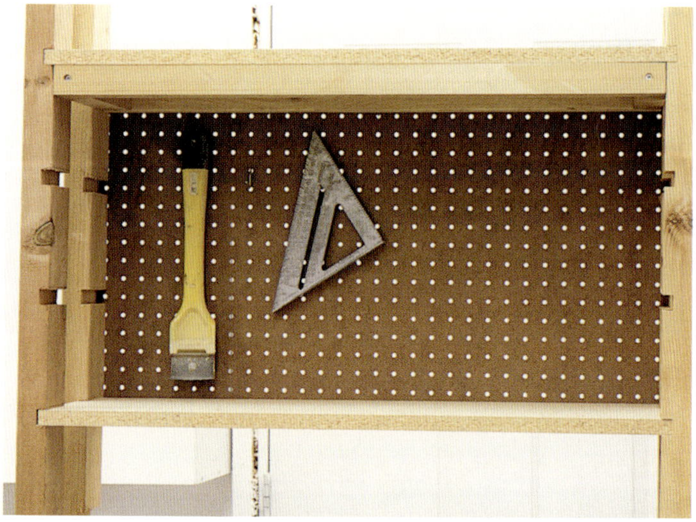

5 Cut the number of adjustable shelves needed. You can also add pegboard between two shelves to store tools and brushes. The shelf unit can be painted or left unfinished when using pressure-treated or cedar lumber.

PROJECT 3

closet storage

In this project, I'll try to provide you with a few ideas that will help improve storage in your closets. Detailing exact measurements would be of little value as everyone's closet is different, but I'll attempt to show you how to add valuable space and organization to any closet.

Each closet is unique, but the construction steps used to build towers, drawers, adjustable shelves and support and divider panels are the same for any closet space; only the sizes are different. The closet I converted is common to many homes that have been built in the last thirty years. Home builders create this style of closet by installing sliding doors across the width of a room. Most are 2' deep with floor-to-ceiling doors, or with doors attached to a drywall-covered header, which ride in a track. They may have three or four doors, depending on the room width. These closets waste a great deal of space but are quick and easy to install for the builders.

The interior is normally at the full room height of 8'. Often, the closet has one divider, or center panel, and a rod on each side to hang clothes. The key to improved closet organization is a drawer tower or towers, depending on closet width, with all the other racks, rods and panels attached.

Building a Drawer/Shelf Tower

The center tower with drawers and shelves shown in the photo is the core module with most closet systems. We want to use the valuable space that often goes unused above and below the hanging rod. The example tower shown is only 18" wide, but it creates a tremendous amount of increased storage space for sweaters and other garments.

All other shelves and clothing racks are fixed to the side of this tower and a wall.

1 I used white melamine-coated particleboard (PB) for this project. It's virtually maintenance free and is prefinished. Two sides are cut at $\frac{5}{8}$" x 23" x 86" long and white heat-activated melamine edge tape is applied to the front edges.

2 The top, bottom and fixed section divider boards are $\frac{5}{8}$" by $16\frac{3}{4}$" wide by 23" deep. Apply edge tape and use three 2" screws per side on each support. The screws should be designed to join PB. Remember to predrill the screw holes and drive them in until the head is flush with the outside surface. The lowest support is $2\frac{3}{8}$" up from the bottom, the middle support is at 51", and the top support is flush with the top edge of the tower sides.

SHOP TIP

Drive screws so the heads are flush to the surface. Use white screw cover caps or stick-on white cover dots that are available at the home center to hide the screw.

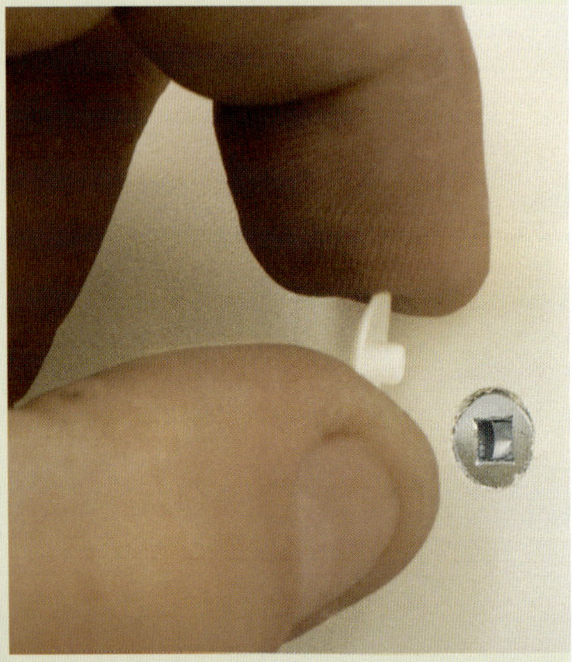

3 The toe kickboard is ⅝" thick by 2⅜" high by 16¾" long. It's secured with one screw on each side and two through the top of the bottom shelf. Set the kickboard 2" back from the front edge.

4 Two backboards, one at ⅝" by 16¾" wide by 33⅝" high and the other at ⅝" by 3" high by 16¾" wide, are attached to strengthen the cabinet. Use 2" screws driven through the side panels and cover caps to secure the boards.

5 The tower will be anchored to the wall with 3" screws through these backboards. Full-height backboards are required on any open shelf section. Drawer compartments need only a small fixing cleat that can be used to secure the cabinet to the wall. That completes the case construction for the tower.

Joinery Techniques

6 These sample drawers are sized to fit an 18"-wide tower using 5⁄8" thick material with an inside width of 16 3⁄4". You'll need the following 5⁄8"-thick panels to build four drawers:

- 8 sides @ 10" high by 22" deep
- 8 backs & fronts @ 10" high by 14 1⁄2" wide
- 4 bottoms @ 15 3⁄4" wide by 22" long
- 4 drawer fronts @ 12 1⁄8" high by 18" wide

Apply edge tape to the exposed edges, which are the tops of the sides, backs and fronts, as well as the side edges of the bottoms. Attach the sides to the backs and fronts with 2" screws. This is a common screw butt joint using 5⁄8"- or 3⁄4"-thick melamine-covered particleboard.

SHOP TIP

You may want a different combination of drawers in your tower. Calculating drawer face height and box heights is easy if you follow a couple of simple rules. First, measure the space available for drawer boxes. In the example tower, we have 49 1⁄4" of free space from the top of the middle board to the lower edge of the bottom board. Drawer faces overlap the middle and bottom board edges, so their thickness is included in the free-space dimension.

Decide on the number of drawers you want and the size of the drawer faces. The total height of the drawer faces, plus a 1⁄16" gap between them, should equal the total free space. For example, if I need three large drawers, my faces will be 16 3⁄8" each (16 3⁄8" times 3 plus the two 1⁄16" spaces between drawers for a total of 49 1⁄4"). Drawer box heights are 2" less than the drawer face height and installed 2" apart. Therefore, the drawer box runners are mounted by attaching the lowest one tight to the bottom board, the next at 16 3⁄8" from the bottom board, and the top one at 32 3⁄4" above the bottom board's top surface.

The bottom drawer face is installed first, and its bottom edge is flush with the lower edge of the bottom board. Use these calculations to determine drawer face and box heights. Any combination of drawer sizes and any number of drawers can be installed.

7 Install the bottom with 2" screws approximately 6" apart.

8 Install a set of 22" bottom-mount drawer glides on each box. Start by installing the runners on the box, then attach the cabinet runners with 12" spacing. I made my drawer box 1" narrower than the inside tower width, according to the specifications with the Blum glides I'm using. However, don't assume this dimension is standard with all manufacturers. Purchase the drawer glides before beginning construction to determine the required clearance.

9 Secure the drawer front to the drawer box with two 1" screws by driving them through the drawer box and into the back of the drawer face. Mount the bottom drawer first as shown, covering the bottom board's edge. Continue attaching the drawer fronts from bottom to top, leaving a $\frac{1}{16}$" space between them.

Drilling Shelf Holes

10 The shelves will be sitting on adjustable pins. Make a drill template from scrap wood, spacing the guide holes 2" or 3" apart. Use the template as shown to drill holes in the upper section of the drawer tower.

SHOP TIP

Make a drill stop using a piece of wood dowel rod. Set it to the template's thickness plus the depth required for the shelf pins you are using, for perfectly drilled holes. More importantly, the stop prevents the drill from being pushed through the cabinet side.

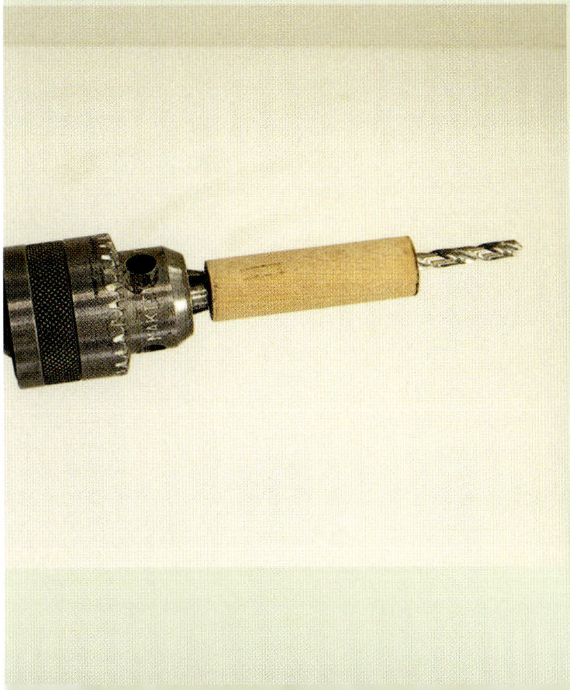

11 Cut the number of shelves you require at $\frac{5}{8}$" by $16\frac{11}{16}$" wide by $22\frac{1}{4}$" deep. Notice that the shelves are slightly narrower than the cabinet's interior so they can be easily adjusted. Cover the front edge with iron-on edge tape or a $\frac{5}{8}$" plastic cap moulding that's secured with construction adhesive. Plastic cap molding is a common shelf edge material that's available at all home centers. It's more durable than iron-on edge tape and an ideal covering for shelf edges that tend to get bumped as items are taken on and off the shelves.

Installing the Closet System

The lead photograph shows another tower in this completed project. This narrow tower, a simple tall cabinet with a melamine door, is a special-application storage tower for tall narrow items and isn't commonly used in most closet systems. Normally, a divider panel is installed to support an additional shelf system for shoes, as well as the hanging rods.

Towers with doors are built following the same construction steps. The door normally covers the top and bottom board edges and is attached with hidden hinges. Doors are 1" wider than the cabinet's inside dimension, as detailed in chapters one and two of this book.

12 Start the closet installation with the drawer tower. Verify that it's level and plumb. Anchor the tower to the wall, through the backboards and into the studs if possible, with 3" screws.

13 You can install any number of divider panels in the closet system. Secure these panels in place with right-angle brackets attached to the floor, ceiling and back wall.

14 I have added an additional column of shelves between an installed divider panel and the tower side. Use the shelf hole jig and procedures described under "Drilling Shelf Holes" for the adjustable shelf pins. These extra shelves can be any width, depending on where the divider panel is installed.

15 Commercially available hanging rods can be purchased at all home stores. These can be adjusted to any width and are attached to the walls and divider panels with screws. I suggest you make square blocks of melamine PB to mount the rods so that you can use longer screws for added support.

CONSTRUCTION NOTES

The lead photograph for this project illustrates a typical layout. The man's side of the closet has two hanging rods, one directly above the other. This configuration is suitable for shirts, pants and jackets. Notice that the woman's side of the closet requires a full-length section to accommodate long dresses.

SONY

Corner Entertainment Center

I've wanted a corner entertainment center ever since I built my family room addition. However, I wasn't able to find one that suited my needs. First, the center had to contain the normal items such as a TV, stereo, VCR and DVD player. But I also wanted storage for VCR tapes, DVDs and compact discs as well as a drawer for the spare cables, cleaning materials, and literature that were necessary to maintain my equipment. After many weeks of searching, I decided to design and build one myself. Here is the result. If you're looking for a great corner unit with plenty of storage space, then look at this project.

A word of caution is in order before you start building this cabinet. Make certain you have enough clearance through doorways in your home to move the cabinet. It's large and can be awkward to move. This project is made with solid oak and oak veneer particleboard. However, any solid wood and sheet material will work just as well.

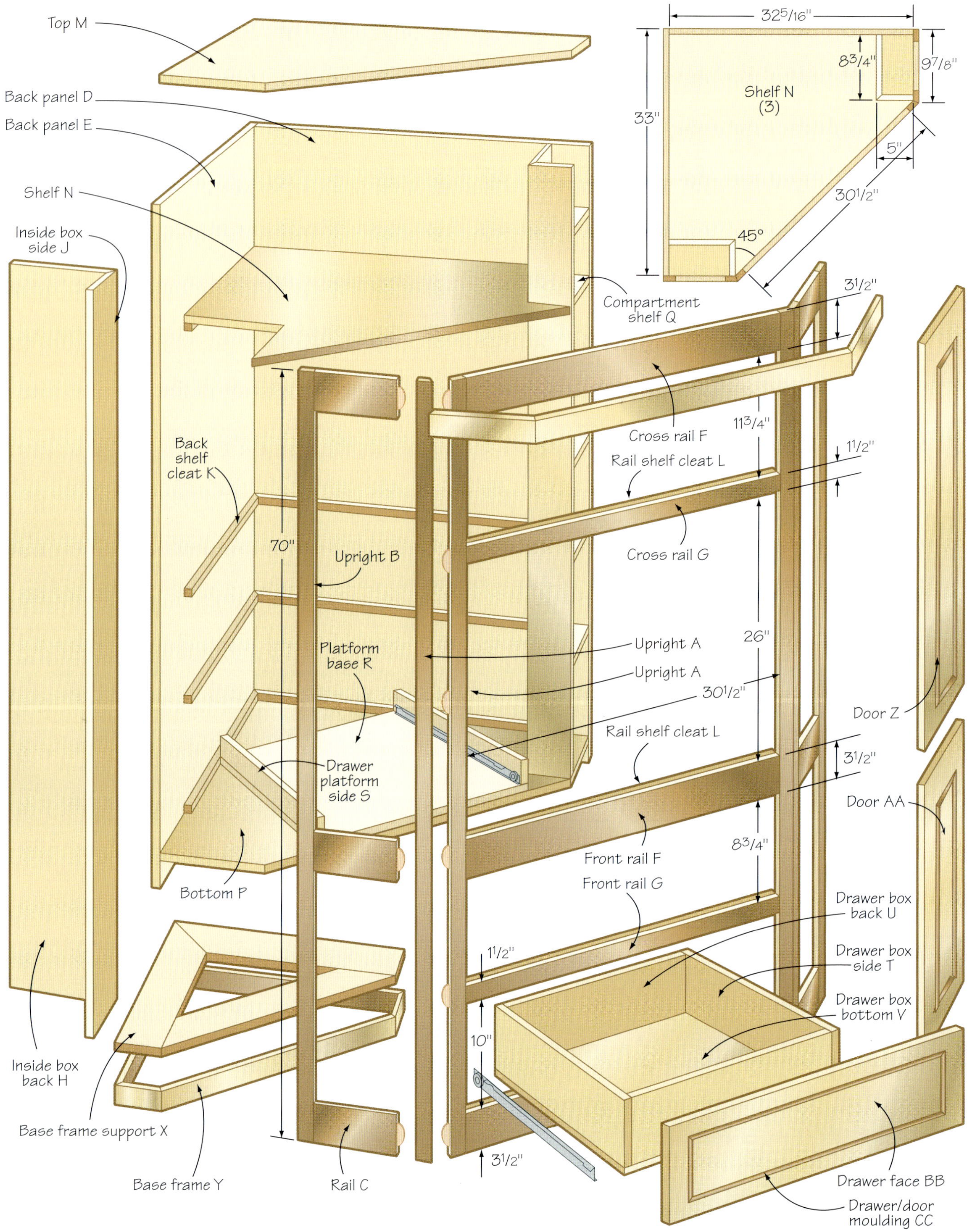
Top M
Back panel D
Back panel E
Shelf N
Inside box side J
32 5/16"
33"
8 3/4"
9 7/8"
Shelf N (3)
5"
30 1/2"
45°
Compartment shelf Q
3 1/2"
Back shelf cleat K
70"
Cross rail F
11 3/4"
1 1/2"
Rail shelf cleat L
Cross rail G
Upright B
Platform base R
Upright A
Upright A
26"
30 1/2"
Door Z
Rail shelf cleat L
Drawer platform side S
3 1/2"
Door AA
Front rail F
8 3/4"
Bottom P
Front rail G
Drawer box back U
1 1/2"
Drawer box side T
Drawer box bottom V
10"
Inside box back H
Base frame support X
3 1/2"
Base frame Y
Rail C
Drawer face BB
Drawer/door moulding CC

INCHES (MILLIMETERS)

REFERENCE	QUANTITY	PART	STOCK	THICKNESS	(mm)	WIDTH	(mm)	LENGTH	(mm)	COMMENTS
A	4	front uprights	solid wood	$^3/_4$	(19)	$1^3/_8$	(35)	70	(1778)	
B	2	rear uprights	solid wood	$^3/_4$	(19)	$1^1/_2$	(38)	70	(1778)	
C	6	rails	solid wood	$^3/_4$	(19)	$3^1/_2$	(89)	7	(178)	
D	1	back panel	veneer PB	$^{11}/_{16}$	(18)	$32^5/_{16}$	(821)	70	(1778)	
E	1	back panel	veneer PB	$^{11}/_{16}$	(18)	33	(838)	70	(1778)	
F	3	front rails	solid wood	$^3/_4$	(19)	$3^1/_2$	(89)	$30^1/_2$	(775)	
G	2	front rails	solid wood	$^3/_4$	(19)	$1^1/_2$	(38)	$30^1/_2$	(775)	
H	2	inside box backs	veneer PB	$^{11}/_{16}$	(18)	$8^3/_4$	(222)	$67^1/_2$	(1715)	
J	2	inside box sides	veneer PB	$^{11}/_{16}$	(18)	5	(127)	$67^1/_2$	(1715)	
K	8	back cleats	solid wood	$^3/_4$	(19)	$^3/_4$	(19)	27	(686)	
L	4	rail shelf cleats	solid wood	$^3/_4$	(19)	$^3/_4$	(19)	$30^1/_2$	(775)	
M	1	top	veneer PB	$^{11}/_{16}$	(18)	36	(914)	36	(914)	
N	3	shelves	veneer PB	$^{11}/_{16}$	(18)	33	(838)	33	(838)	
P	1	bottom	veneer PB	$^{11}/_{16}$	(18)	33	(838)	33	(838)	
Q	12	compartment shelves	PB	$^3/_4$	(19)	$4^1/_4$	(108)	$7^7/_8$	(200)	
R	1	platform base	PB	$^3/_4$	(19)	22	(559)	18	(457)	
S	2	platform sides	PB	$^3/_4$	(19)	2	(51)	18	(457)	
T	2	drawer box sides	veneer PB	$^{11}/_{16}$	(18)	$8^1/_{16}$	(205)	18	(457)	
U	2	drawer box front & back	veneer PB	$^{11}/_{16}$	(18)	$8^1/_{16}$	(205)	$18^1/_8$	(460)	
V	1	drawer box bottom	veneer PB	$^{11}/_{16}$	(18)	$19^1/_2$	(496)	18	(457)	
W		top trim	solid wood	$^3/_4$	(19)	$1^1/_2$	(38)	5'	(1.5m)	mitered and cut to length as detailed in the text
X		base frame support	softwood	$1^1/_2$	(38)	$3^1/_2$	(89)	8'	(2.4m)	mitered and cut to length as detailed in the text
Y		base frame	solid wood	$^3/_4$	(19)	$3^1/_2$	(89)	10'	(3m)	mitered and cut to length as detailed in the text
Z	2	upper doors	veneer PB	$^{11}/_{16}$	(18)	8	(203)	$41^1/_4$	(1048)	
AA	2	lower doors	veneer PB	$^{11}/_{16}$	(18)	8	(203)	$22^1/_4$	(565)	
BB	1	drawer face	veneer PB	$^{11}/_{16}$	(18)	12	(305)	$22^1/_4$	(565)	
CC		door/drawer moulding	solid wood							as chosen

HARDWARE & SUPPLIES

wood veneer edge tape
1 set–18" (457mm) bottom-mount drawer glides
$1^1/_4$" (32mm) PB screws
$1^1/_2$" (38mm) PB screws
2" (51mm) PB screws
drawer/door pulls
8–door hinges
wood plugs
brad nails
corner round moulding
glue
#10 biscuits
finishing nails

1 Cut four front uprights A from solid wood and rip an angled edge at $22\frac{1}{2}$° as shown.

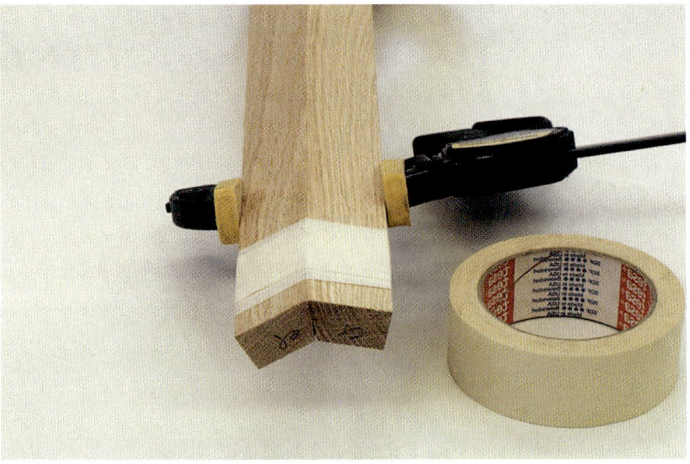

2 Join the uprights A with glue and biscuits to form two front corner posts. It's difficult to hold the uprights together during assembly. To help hold the pieces, wrap tape tightly around the assembly after inserting the biscuits and applying the glue. The important joint is the outside angle as it will be visible, so get it as tight as possible.

3 To form the sides, attach three oak rails C to each rear upright B at the positions shown in the illustration. Two assemblies are required. The simplest method of attaching the rails to the uprights is with 2" screws through the upright B into the rail ends. Counterbore the screw holes and fill with wood plugs.

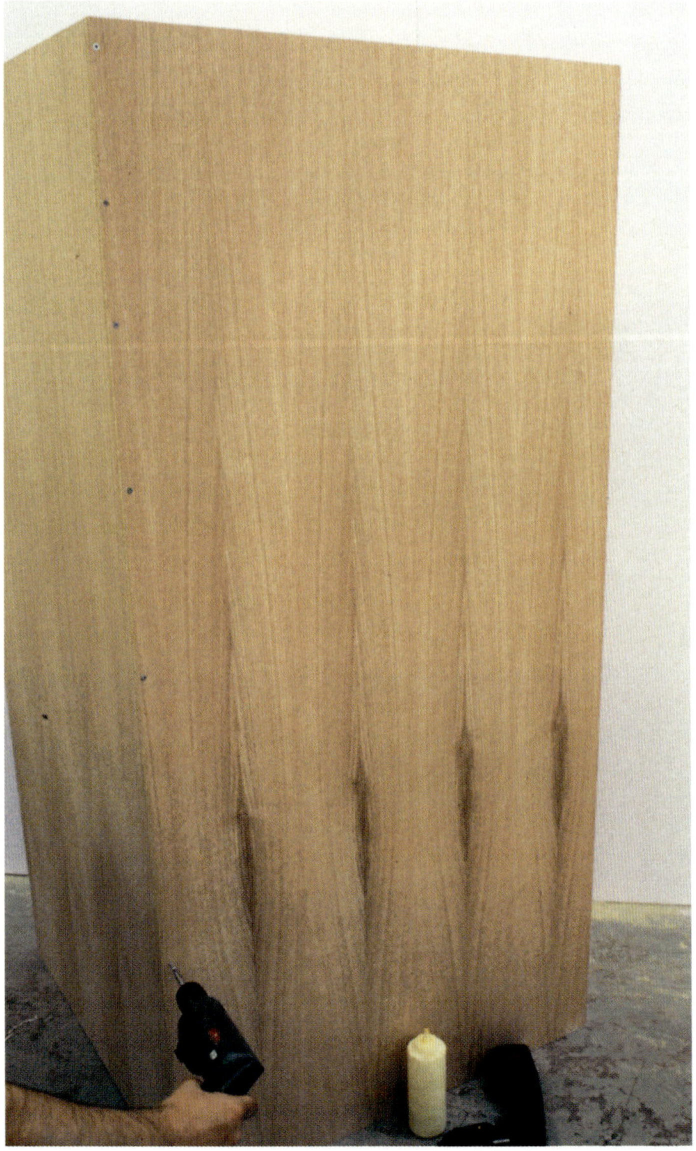

4 Join the angled upright assemblies, made with two front uprights A, to the side frame rails C, using dowels or biscuits and glue. Clamp the frame assembly together until the glue sets. Cut the two back panels D and E as shown in the materials list. Use glue and 2" screws to join the panels, forming a right angle that measures 33" on each outside face. Notice that panel D is $32\frac{5}{16}$" wide so the total width will equal the $\frac{11}{16}$" thick panel E width when they are joined with a 90° butt joint.

5 Join the side frame assemblies to the back panels D and E. Use glue and four 2" screws in counterbored holes through the front of the face frame rear uprights B into the back panel edges. Plug the holes with the appropriate wood plugs.

SHOP TIP

As the construction proceeds, certain corners must remain at 90° during the assembly. A typical example is the right-angle joint for the back panels. Temporarily clamp 90° corner blocks in place to maintain those angles until they are supported.

6 Next, install the three front rails F and two front rails G in the positions shown in the illustration. My rails are set so a 27" TV will fit in the center section. If you have another application, simply change the back panels D and E as well as the widths of rails F and G to achieve the required front opening width. All my rails are $30\frac{1}{2}$" long. Be sure to have the side frames to back panel joint as well as the back panel to back panel joint blocked at 90°. Verify your measurement, as it may vary slightly because of small dimensional differences when cutting the side frame members. It's not critically important for the rails to be exactly $30\frac{1}{2}$" wide. It is, however, important that the 90° corners be accurate when taking rail length measurements. Install the rails with dowels or biscuit joints. You may need a helping hand at this point to get the rails to frame joints set, glued and clamped.

7 The side and back panel assembly for the storage compartments are built with the $^{11}/_{16}$" veneer PB inside box backs H and inside box sides J. Cut one edge of each panel with a 45° angle to form the corner. Join with glue and finishing nails. Put the boxes in place and secure with glue and 2" screws through the face frame into the box sides J and through the cabinet back panels D and E into the edge on the box backs H. Install the boxes so their upper edges are flush with the top edge of the cabinet.

8 The three middle shelves N and bottom P will be supported with $^3/_4$" square wood back cleats K on the back panels D and E and rail shelf cleats L behind the front rails F and G. The photograph shows the cleats in position. However, this is only to show the installation procedures. Install the cleats as you fit the shelves. You'll need a clear path to slide the shelves in place from the top of the cabinet. All the cleats, with the exception of the bottom support cleats (see next step for bottom cleats' positions), are installed so the $^{11}/_{16}$"-thick shelves will rest $^1/_8$" below their respective rail's top edge. All the shelves are cut by placing them on top of the cabinet and tracing the outline. There are three separate shelf patterns. The bottom P is cut to the inside perimeter of the cabinet, ignoring the compartment boxes. The middle three shelves N are also cut to the inside perimeter of the cabinet, with a notch cut for the outside perimeter of the storage compartment boxes. And the top M is the same pattern as the outside perimeter of the cabinet. Attach the cleats K and L with glue and $1^1/_4$"-long screws.

9 Trace the outline for the bottom P and cut it to size as detailed in step 8. Install the shelf cleats K and L above the shelf position, flush with the bottom edges of the compartment boxes. The bottom P will also be the bottom for the storage compartments formed by boards H and J. One cleat K is on each back panel D and E and the third cleat L is behind the front rail F. Install the bottom P by securing it with glue and screws to the cleats. The cleats for this shelf are installed above the board because the force from the base frame will be pushing upward on the bottom P as well as the cleats K and L.

10 Trace the pattern for the middle shelves N, as described in step 8, and cut as accurately as possible. Install the cleats K and L for each shelf in order, then slide in the shelf from the top. If the shelf isn't cut clean or is damaged from angle cutting the veneer board, use quarter-round as shown around the shelf perimeter and double-edge rounded-over flat moulding to hide any imperfections where the shelf meets the front rail.

11 Round over the inside and outside edges of the cabinet, using a router equipped with a $\frac{3}{8}$" roundover bit. Do not round over the cabinet top edge. Cut as many compartment shelves Q as required for your storage application. I will be storing videocassettes, but you may prefer to store compact discs or DVDs. I've installed six shelves per side, spaced approximately 10" apart. Secure them in place with glue and 2" finishing nails through the cabinet back panels D and E, as well as the compartment side J and back H.

12 The cabinet is angled, which means a platform must be constructed to support the drawer runners. Build a flat platform with platform base R and sides S for the bottom-mount drawer glides. The $\frac{3}{4}$"-thick drawer platform dimensions are shown in the materials list. Join the sides to the platform base with glue and $1\frac{1}{2}$" wood screws as shown. Install drawer runners and screw the platform in place. It's installed directly behind the bottom rail F, resting on the bottom shelf cleats K and L. Use $1\frac{1}{2}$" wood screws to secure the platform to the cleats. Center the drawer platform in the middle of the opening.

13 Cut and assemble a simple drawer box, using panels T, U and V, that's 18" deep and 19½" wide. Apply edge tape to the top edges of T and U, as well as the side edges of the bottom V. The sides T are joined to the front and back U with a butt joint using 1½" wood screws and glue. The bottom V is also secured with glue and 2" PB screws.

14 Attach the bottom-mount drawer glides and verify that the drawer operates properly. The drawer box must be 1" narrower than the inside rail-to-rail dimension of the drawer platform.

15 Cut the top M at 36" square. Lay it on top of the cabinet and trace the outside cabinet perimeter on the board. Cut it to the new dimensions, following the traced lines. Attach it to the top of the cabinet using glue and finishing nails.

16 Round over the upper and lower edges of the top trim W, on the front face only. Cut the necessary angles and attach the pieces to the cabinet top M front and side faces with glue and finishing nails.

17 This cabinet will have a $3\frac{1}{2}$"-high base frame installed that's set back $3\frac{1}{2}$" from the cabinet's outside perimeter. The frame is made with $3\frac{1}{2}$"-wide oak boards Y on their edges and a 2x4 frame support X using construction lumber installed on its wide face. Draw an outline on the bottom of the cabinet $4\frac{1}{4}$" back from the outside perimeter and attach 2x4 frame supports X after angle cutting to length. Secure $3\frac{1}{2}$"-wide base frames Y on their edge to the frame supports X after cutting to the correct angles and lengths.

18 I am using $\frac{11}{16}$" veneer PB with edge tape to make my slab-style doors Z and AA as well as the drawer face BB. To add detail, 1"-wide moulding CC is attached to the doors and drawer faces 1" in from all edges. Drill the necessary holes to run wires from each compartment, as well as a hole in the bottom for the power supply. Sand and finish the cabinet. I applied three coats of oil-based polyurethane.

television armoire | *page 108*

large dresser | *page 116*

Efficient Master Bedroom Furniture

bedside cabinet and bookcase | ***page 121***

This series of projects is one of my favorite woodworking creations in the last few years. I wanted a strong and functional bedroom set for my home without any fancy curves or carvings. It had to be practical, and I didn't want to spend a fortune on materials.

The complete project set has been in my home for a while and I'm still pleased with the design; I wouldn't change a thing. The armoire has a 27" TV installed with a VCR and has two large storage drawers for clothes. The matching dresser has more than enough room for clothing and ample space on the top for accessories and display items.

The bedside cabinet provides enough room for a phone and bedside lamp, as well as shelves for books and collectibles. The two large drawers in each unit are a real bonus and add a lot of found storage space for clothing.

I'm still enjoying everything about this bedroom set, and I hope you'll find it suits your requirements. I don't think you'll find a more practical or cost-effective bedroom furniture set.

PROJECT 1

television armoire

This project is the start of a series of similarly styled bedroom storage furniture. The television armoire is now a popular item in most large bedrooms. Nothing is nicer than enjoying your morning coffee in bed while watching TV. But that ugly television, with all the necessary wires and equipment, is a real eyesore. This cabinet will provide hidden storage for the TV and give you a couple of large storage drawers as a bonus.

The only difference between this and the other cabinets I'll build for the bedroom is the use of inset doors. They're necessary because we want to hide the doors inside the cabinet when watching television. Don't let the complex-looking doors stop you from building this. It's just a matter of putting sticks and panels together — one piece at a time.

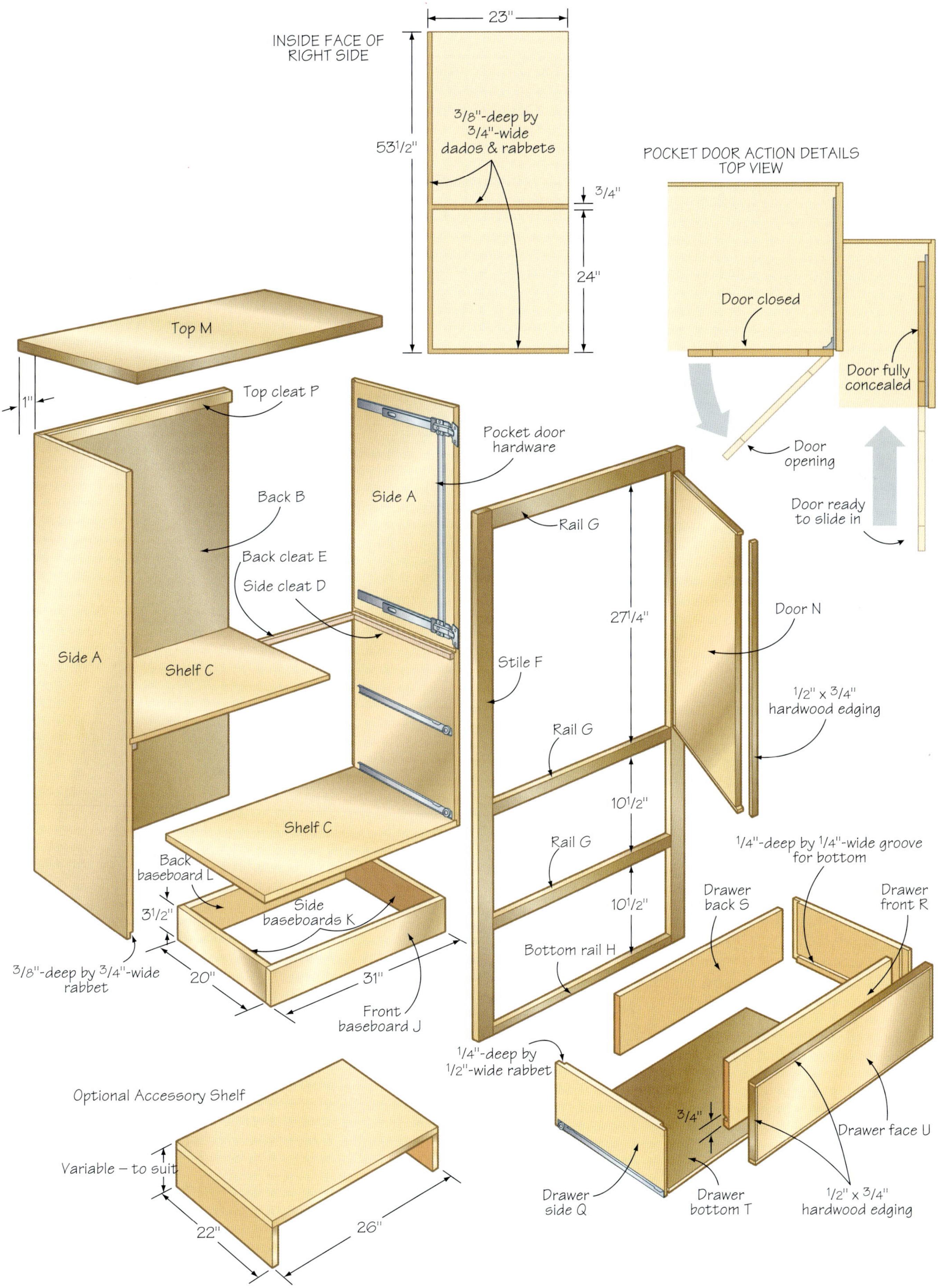
INSIDE FACE OF RIGHT SIDE
23"
53 1/2"
3/8"-deep by 3/4"-wide dados & rabbets
3/4"
24"
POCKET DOOR ACTION DETAILS TOP VIEW
Door closed
Door fully concealed
Door opening
Door ready to slide in
Top M
1"
Top cleat P
Pocket door hardware
Back B
Side A
Back cleat E
Side cleat D
Side A
Shelf C
Rail G
27 1/4"
Door N
Stile F
1/2" x 3/4" hardwood edging
Rail G
10 1/2"
Shelf C
Rail G
Back baseboard L
1/4"-deep by 1/4"-wide groove for bottom
3 1/2"
Side baseboards K
10 1/2"
Drawer back S
Drawer front R
3/8"-deep by 3/4"-wide rabbet
20"
31"
Bottom rail H
Front baseboard J
1/4"-deep by 1/2"-wide rabbet
Optional Accessory Shelf
3/4"
Drawer face U
Variable – to suit
Drawer side Q
Drawer bottom T
1/2" x 3/4" hardwood edging
22"
26"

INCHES (MILLIMETERS)

REFERENCE	QUANTITY	PART	STOCK	THICKNESS	(mm)	WIDTH	(mm)	LENGTH	(mm)	COMMENTS
A	2	sides	veneer PB	$^3/_4$	(19)	23	(584)	$53^1/_2$	(1359)	
B	1	back	veneer PB	$^3/_4$	(19)	$33^1/_4$	(845)	$53^1/_2$	(1359)	
C	2	shelves	veneer PB	$^3/_4$	(19)	$33^1/_4$	(845)	$22^1/_4$	(565)	
D	2	side cleats	solid wood	$^3/_4$	(19)	$^3/_4$	(19)	$22^1/_4$	(565)	
E	1	back cleat	solid wood	$^3/_4$	(19)	$^3/_4$	(19)	31	(787)	
F	2	stiles	solid wood	$^3/_4$	(19)	$1^1/_2$	(38)	$53^1/_2$	(1359)	
G	3	rails	solid wood	$^3/_4$	(19)	$1^1/_2$	(38)	31	(787)	
H	1	bottom rail	solid wood	$^3/_4$	(19)	$^3/_4$	(19)	31	(787)	
J	1	front base board	solid wood	$^3/_4$	(19)	$3^1/_2$	(89)	31	(787)	
K	2	side base boards	solid wood	$^3/_4$	(19)	$3^1/_2$	(89)	20	(508)	
L	1	back base board	solid wood	$^3/_4$	(19)	$3^1/_2$	(89)	$29^1/_2$	(749)	
M	1	top	solid wood	1	(25)	36	(914)	25	(635)	$^3/_4$"(19mm) thick tops can also be used
N	2	doors	veneer PB	$^3/_4$	(19)	$15^3/_8$	(391)	27	(686)	door faces are $^3/_4$"(19mm) PB banded with $^3/_4$" x $^1/_2$" (19mm x 13mm) solid wood
P	1	top cleat	solid wood	$^3/_4$	(19)	$1^1/_2$	(38)	$32^1/_2$	(826)	
DRAWERS										
Q	4	sides	birch ply	$^1/_2$	(13)	$9^1/_2$	(241)	22	(559)	
R	2	fronts	birch ply	$^1/_2$	(13)	$9^1/_2$	(241)	$29^1/_2$	(749)	
S	2	backs	birch ply	$^1/_2$	(13)	$8^3/_4$	(222)	$29^1/_2$	(749)	
T	2	bottoms	plywood	$^1/_2$	(13)	$21^3/_4$	(552)	$29^1/_2$	(749)	
U	2	drawer faces	veneer PB	$^3/_4$	(19)	$11^1/_2$	(292)	32	(813)	drawer faces are $^3/_4$"(19mm) PB banded with $^3/_4$" x $^1/_2$" (19mm x 13mm) solid wood

HARDWARE & SUPPLIES

1–22" (559mm) pocket door hardware set
2–22" (559mm) drawer glide sets
2" (51mm) PB screws
$1^1/_4$" (32mm) PB screws
2" (51mm) finishing nails
glue
4–door and drawer handles
wood plugs
2" (51mm) wood screws
brad nails
wood edge tape
1" (25mm) screws

1 The two sides A require a rabbet cut that's $^3/_4$" wide by $^3/_8$" deep on the inside back face and one on the bottom edge of each inside face. Next, cut a $^3/_8$" deep by $^3/_4$" wide dado 24" up from the bottom edge of each panel to accept the middle fixed shelf C.

2 Apply glue to the back rabbets on the sides A and clamp the back B between the side boards in the rabbets. Secure the back with 2" finishing nails through the back face of B and into the edges of the side boards. The nails will hold back B in the rabbets until the adhesive sets. Cut the bottom and middle shelf C to the size listed in the materials list. Glue and nail the bottom shelf in place by nailing from the bottom face into the side boards. Use 2" screws through the backboard into the bottom shelf as well. Clamp the middle shelf in the dado. Install cleats D and E under the middle shelf to provide added support for a television and other related equipment, which will rest on this shelf. Secure the cleats with glue and $1^1/_4$" screws into sides A, back B and middle shelf C. Install 2" screws through the back B into shelf C.

3 Cut the two stiles F (vertical face frame members) and secure to the front of the case with glue and 2" finishing nails. Align the outside edge of the stiles with the outside faces of the cabinet sides A. Secure the rails G and H in the positions shown with glue and 2" screws. Predrill and counterbore the screw holes through the stiles F and fill with a wood plug. You can also use 2" finishing nails, on the face of the rail and into the shelf, where the bottom and middle rails meet the shelves. Sand the face frame and round over the outside edge of the two stiles and the outside edge of the bottom rail.

4 The cabinet base is a simple support made from solid oak boards that are 3⁄4" thick by 3½" high. The base is strong and provides toekick space as well as a recess at the cabinet back that will fit over most baseboard mouldings. This feature allows the cabinet to be placed tightly against a wall. Cut the base frames J, K and L to the sizes listed. The pieces are glued and screwed together using 2" long screws in counterbored holes that are filled with wood plugs. The outside dimension of the frame for the TV Armoire is 20¾" deep by 31" wide. Draw a line around the bottom of the cabinet baseboard 1½" from each edge. Set the square at 2¼" and draw the inner perimeter line. This will outline the base frame position.

SHOP TIP

The easiest way to cut rabbets, dadoes and grooves on large sheets is by using a stacked carbide dado blade set on the table saw.

5 Before attaching the base frame to the cabinet, drill small holes through the base cabinet in the middle of the frame outline. Space the holes about 6" apart. Next, apply glue to the frame and clamp it in place. The pencil outline will help you clamp it in the proper position. Use the pilot holes that appear through the cabinet base as a guide to drill holes through the baseboard and into the frame edges. Install 2" wood screws in each hole, making sure the frame is drawn tight against the underside of the baseboard.

6 I will be using a hardwood-edged oak veneer particle board door. The inset door needs clearance on its top and bottom edge. Therefore, the overall height of each door will be 27". They also need side and middle clearance, so the doors will be $15\frac{3}{8}$" wide. That will provide a little better than $\frac{1}{16}$" at each side and between the doors. Cut the two oak veneer door panels N. Next, cut two $\frac{3}{4}$"-thick hardwood strips $\frac{1}{2}$" wide by 26" long and two at $15\frac{3}{8}$" long. Attach the strips to the door edges with glue and brad nails, so the finished size of each door is $15\frac{3}{8}$" wide by 27" high. Then, round over all the face edges with a $\frac{1}{4}$" roundover router bit.

SHOP TIP

This procedure of building a base frame and installing it on the cabinets will be used for all the cabinets in this section. The only change will be the outside dimensions of the frame. If the cabinet happens to be located over a floor heating register, a grill can be installed in the frame. This was the case with my dresser, as you'll see in the photograph at the beginning of that project.

7 I am using 22" pocket door hardware manufactured by Blum. The manufacturer supplies all the necessary installation instructions, and I recommend you follow their procedures.

8 Installing the pocket door hardware can be a skill-testing project. However, take your time and follow the installation steps carefully.

9 Cut the top M to a finished size of 25" deep by 36" wide. Use a $\frac{3}{8}$" roundover bit on the front and side edges. Clamp the top in place, so the top's back edge is flush with the rear face of back B, and draw a line where the inside face of the back meets the top. Install the top cleat P on that line with screws in holes twice the diameter of the screw shaft so the top can expand and contract. Don't overdrive the screws, so the top can move.

10 Clamp the top in its proper location with a 1" overhang on the sides and a $1\frac{1}{4}$" overhang on the front edge. The top should be flush with the outside face of the back B. Predrill holes twice the diameter of the screw shafts and secure the top from the underside of the front rail G and face of the top cleat P. The screws should be snug but not tight, as mentioned in step 9, so the top can move if necessary.

11 The only additional accessory you will have to make is an interior shelf. The height is determined by the television. My shelf is 26" wide by 9" high, but many will be different, which is why the shelf panels aren't detailed in the materials list. The shelf is $\frac{3}{4}$"-thick particleboard with wood edge tape applied to the visible edges. Build the shelf 22" deep so wires and cables can be connected between the TV and any other equipment in your cabinet. The only items left to build are the drawers. Use the sizes specified in the materials list and follow the procedures detailed in the following "Building Traditional Birch Plywood Drawers for Bottom-Mount Glides."

shop talk | ***Building Traditional Birch Plywood Drawers***

All the projects in this chapter will have drawers built of $\frac{1}{2}$"-thick cabinet-grade plywood. You'll come across a few different names for this plywood, which is sometimes known as Baltic or Russian birch. But no matter what it's called in your area, it has one important feature. It should have void-free layers. Simply stated, all the layers should be free of holes or defects.

Keep a couple of details in mind when building this type of drawer box. The dimensions are based on the Blum bottom-mount drawer glides. The drawer box is 1" narrower than the opening and 1" less in height. The depth of the box equals the drawer glide length. The drawer face is 1" wider than the opening and 1" greater in height. However, check the specifications for your drawer glides.

1 Cut two drawer sides. Each side will have a $\frac{1}{2}$"- wide by $\frac{1}{4}$"- deep rabbet on each end. The sides will also need a $\frac{1}{4}$"- wide by $\frac{1}{4}$"- deep groove cut with its top edge $\frac{3}{4}$" up from the bottom edge.

2 Cut the drawer front. It has to have a $\frac{1}{4}$"- deep by $\frac{1}{4}$"-wide groove with the top edge of the groove $\frac{3}{4}$" up from the bottom edge. Cut the back board $\frac{3}{4}$" narrower than the front board. No dadoes or rabbets are required. Secure the drawer front to the sides, in the rabbets, using glue and brad nails. Make certain all the grooves are aligned.

3 Attach the drawer back by securing it with glue and brad nails in the rear side board rabbets. Align the drawer back's top edge with the drawer side's top edges, making sure not to cover the grooves.

4 Cut a piece of $\frac{1}{4}$"- thick Birch plywood for the drawer bottom. Slide it into the grooves, which should place it flush with the back face of the drawer back. Secure it to the drawer back's bottom edge with brad nails. Do not use glue anywhere on this board.

5 Install the glides on the drawer box according to the manufacturer's instructions. For face frame applications, such as the ones in this section, we must install $\frac{3}{4}$"- thick by $1\frac{1}{2}$"- wide wood cleats to carry the case glide members straight back from the inside stile edges.

6 Cut a drawer face from $\frac{3}{4}$" oak veneer PB and solid-wood strips as detailed earlier in this chapter. Secure it to the box with four 1" screws from the inside. The drawer face should overlap the opening by $\frac{1}{2}$" on the top, bottom and sides.

PROJECT 2

large dresser

Many of today's dressers never seem to have enough drawer space. We're always looking for more room to store socks, undergarments, sweaters and T-shirts. This dresser project may be the answer to your needs. It's all drawers! It has six wide large-capacity drawers in a dresser that's more than 5' long.

The style of this dresser project matches all the other furniture in this chapters. You can make all of them as a set or any one as a stand-alone unit. The choice is yours.

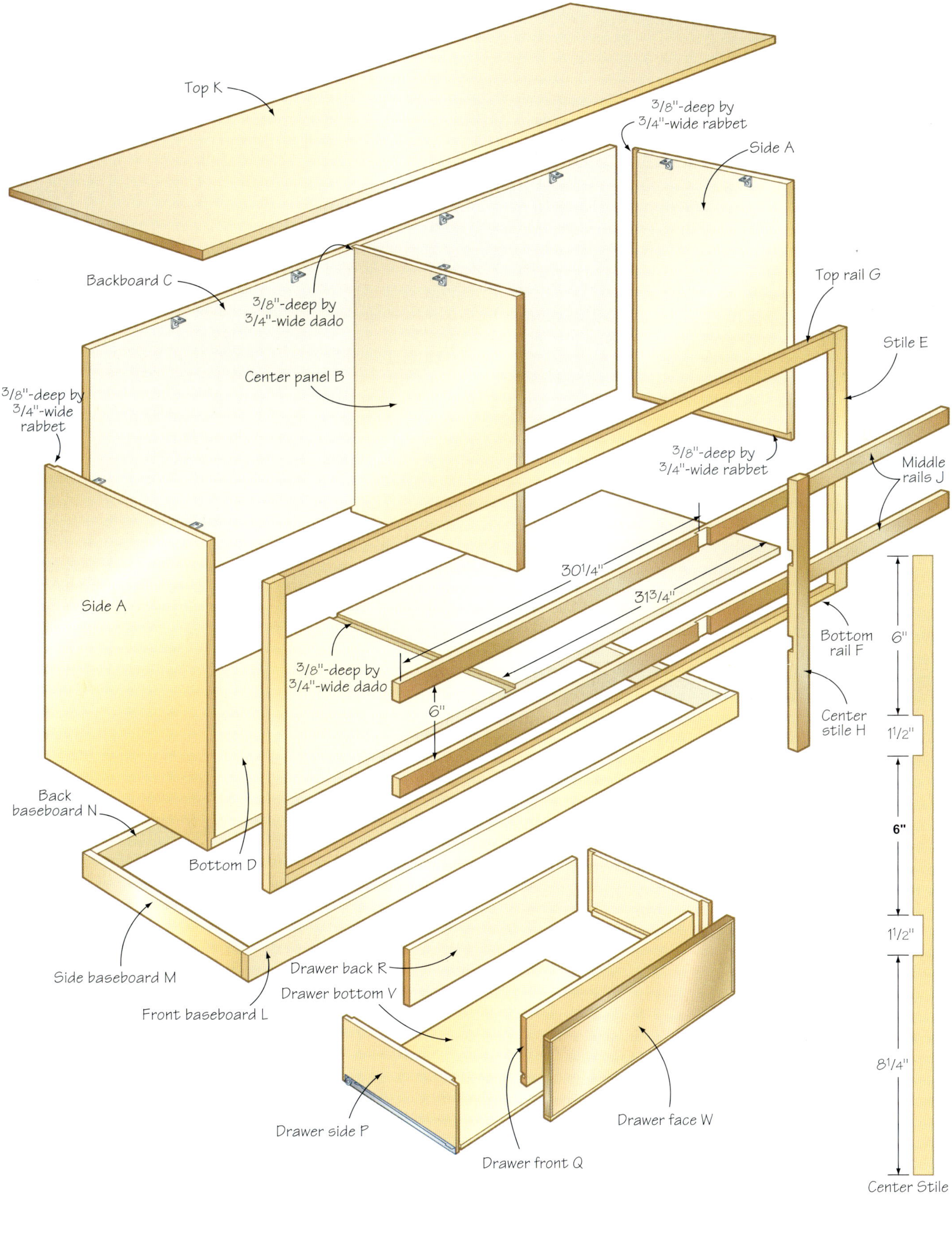
Top K
3/8"-deep by 3/4"-wide rabbet
Side A
Backboard C
3/8"-deep by 3/4"-wide dado
Top rail G
Stile E
3/8"-deep by 3/4"-wide rabbet
Center panel B
3/8"-deep by 3/4"-wide rabbet
Middle rails J
Side A
30 1/4"
31 3/4"
3/8"-deep by 3/4"-wide dado
6"
Bottom rail F
Center stile H
Back baseboard N
Bottom D
Side baseboard M
Front baseboard L
Drawer back R
Drawer bottom V
Drawer side P
Drawer front Q
Drawer face W
6"
1 1/2"
6"
1 1/2"
8 1/4"
Center Stile

INCHES (MILLIMETERS)

REFERENCE	QUANTITY	PART	STOCK	THICKNESS	(mm)	WIDTH	(mm)	LENGTH	(mm)	COMMENTS
A	2	sides	veneer PB	¾	(19)	17½	(445)	25½	(648)	
B	1	center panel	veneer PB	¾	(19)	17⅛	(435)	25⅛	(638)	
C	1	backboard	particleboard	¾	(19)	24¾	(629)	64¼	(1632)	backboard made of nonveneered ¾"(19mm) particleboard
D	1	bottom	particleboard	¾	(19)	17½	(445)	64¼	(1632)	bottom made of nonveneered ¾"(19mm) particleboard
E	2	stiles	hardwood	¾	(19)	1½	(38)	25½	(648)	
F	1	bottom rail	hardwood	¾	(19)	¾	(19)	62	(1575)	
G	1	top rail	hardwood	¾	(19)	1½	(38)	62	(1575)	
H	1	center stile	hardwood	¾	(19)	1½	(38)	23¼	(591)	
J	2	middle rails	hardwood	¾	(19)	1½	(38)	62	(1575)	
K	1	top	hardwood	1	(25)	19¼	(489)	67	(1702)	
L	1	front baseboard	solid wood	¾	(19)	3½	(89)	62	(1575)	
M	2	side baseboards	solid wood	¾	(19)	3½	(89)	14½	(368)	
N	1	back baseboards	solid wood	¾	(19)	3½	(89)	60½	(1537)	
P	8	drawer sides	birch plywood	½	(13)	5	(127)	16	(406)	
Q	4	drawer fronts	birch plywood	½	(13)	5	(127)	28¾	(730)	
R	4	drawer backs	birch plywood	½	(13)	4¼	(108)	28¾	(730)	
S	4	drawer sides	birch plywood	½	(13)	7¼	(184)	16	(406)	
T	2	drawer fronts	birch plywood	½	(13)	7¼	(184)	28¾	(730)	
U	2	drawer backs	birch plywood	½	(13)	6½	(165)	28¾	(730)	
V	6	drawer bottoms	plywood	¼	(6)	15¾	(400)	28¾	(730)	
W	4	drawer faces	veneer PB	¾	(19)	7	(178)	31¼	(794)	drawer faces are ¾"(19mm) PB banded with ¾" x ½" (19mm x 13mm) solid wood
X	2	drawer faces	veneer PB	¾	(19)	9¼	(235)	31¼	(794)	drawer faces are ¾"(19mm) PB banded with ¾" x ½" (19mm x 13mm) solid wood

HARDWARE & SUPPLIES
6–16" (406mm) drawer glide sets
metal countertop clips
2" (51mm) PB screws
finishing nails
glue
6–drawer handles
colored putty
2" (51mm) wood screws
wood plugs
⅝" (16mm) wood screws

1 Cut the two sides A, center panel B, backboard C and bottom D as detailed in the materials list. Panels C and D require a dado that's ¾" wide by ⅜" deep centered on their inside face. The side panels A each require two rabbet cuts that are ¾" wide by ⅜" deep on their rear and bottom inside face edges. Place the bottom D in each side panel bottom rabbet. Use glue, with finishing nails driven through the bottom panel into the edge of the side panels to secure them until the adhesive sets. Be sure the bottom panel's dado is facing toward the cabinet's interior before securing the panels.

2 Place the backboard C in the side panel rabbets, making sure it rests tight against the bottom D. Use glue and finishing nails through the backboard into the sides A to secure the back. Nails should also be driven from the underside of the bottom D into the backboard edge.

3 The center panel B is placed in the aligned dadoes on the backboard C and bottom D. Brush glue in the dadoes, then secure the panel with finishing nails through both back and bottom boards.

4 Cut the two stiles E and attach them to the outside edges of the cabinet with glue and finishing nails. The nail holes are filled with a colored putty stick matching the final finish. Verify that the outside edges of the stiles are flush with the outside edges of the cabinet.

5 Cut and attach the bottom rail F to the cabinet. This rail should cover the edge of bottom D completely. Use glue and finishing nails in drilled holes to secure the rail.

6 The top rail G is attached to the stiles with glue and 2" wood screws in counterbored pilot holes through the stiles E, which will be filled with wood plugs. Glue the center panel B to the rail G and secure with a finishing nail through the rail face. Before nailing, verify that the center panel is correctly positioned. The distance from center panel B to the sides A should be equal on the top and bottom.

SHOP TIP

Temporarily place the middle rails J in their correct position. Use the center stile H as a guide and mark the dado location on each rail. It's more accurate than using a tape measure.

7 The center stile H requires two dadoes cut in the stile where the middle rails J cross. These $1\frac{1}{2}$"-wide by $\frac{3}{8}$"-deep dadoes will form a half-lap joint with the two middle rails once they are dadoed. The center stile H is attached to the center panel B with glue and nails with the dadoes facing out. Verify that there is equal spacing between the center stile H and the two outside stiles E.

8 Cut the two middle rails J to the size shown in the materials list. Both rails require a $\frac{3}{8}$"-deep by $1\frac{1}{2}$"-wide dado in the center so they will fit into the middle stile dadoes, forming half-lap joints. Secure the rails with glue and 3" wood screws through the stiles E at either end of the cabinet, as well as nails through the half-lap joint into the center panel B.

9 Build a base using boards L, M and N. The outside dimension should be $15\frac{1}{4}$" deep by 62" wide. Position it $1\frac{1}{2}$" in from the sides, back and front as detailed in project one, "Television Armoire." Follow the steps outlined in project one to assemble the base frame.

10 Install countertop clips, which are simple right-angle brackets, around the inside perimeter of the cabinet. Place four clips on the back and front, as well as two on each end. Glue up the top K, following the procedures in chapter 1, page 16.

Then, round over the top and bottom edges on the front and two sides of the cabinet top. Place it on the dresser so that there is a 1" overhang on the sides and front edge. Use $\frac{5}{8}$" wood screws, inserted through the holes in the countertop clips, to secure the top but don't overtighten the screws, so the top can expand and contract with changing humidity levels.

Build four drawers that are 5" high by 16" deep and $29\frac{1}{4}$" wide and two bottom drawers $7\frac{1}{4}$" high by 16" deep and $29\frac{1}{4}$" wide. The drawer fronts are $\frac{3}{4}$" thick, and you'll need four at 7" high by $31\frac{1}{4}$" wide and two that are $9\frac{1}{4}$" high by $31\frac{1}{4}$" wide. Follow the techniques detailed previously in this chapter when building and installing Birch plywood drawers and wood-edged drawer faces.

Perform the final sanding and apply your favorite finish. Like all the projects in this section, the dresser was finished with three coats of oil-based semigloss polyurethane.

PROJECT 3

bedside cabinet and bookcase

This combination night table and bookcase is part of the master bedroom storage furniture suite. It has the same style base and top.

The night table is a great addition to the bedroom project and, with two large capacity drawers, provides extra storage. To take advantage of the often unused space above the night table, I've added an upper section with adjustable shelves for even more storage. This shelf section can be used for books or to display your favorite family treasures.

The sides will receive a bottom, top and back panel using the same construction methods as the dresser. The materials list shows the parts needed for one cabinet; double the quantities given if you make two units as I did.

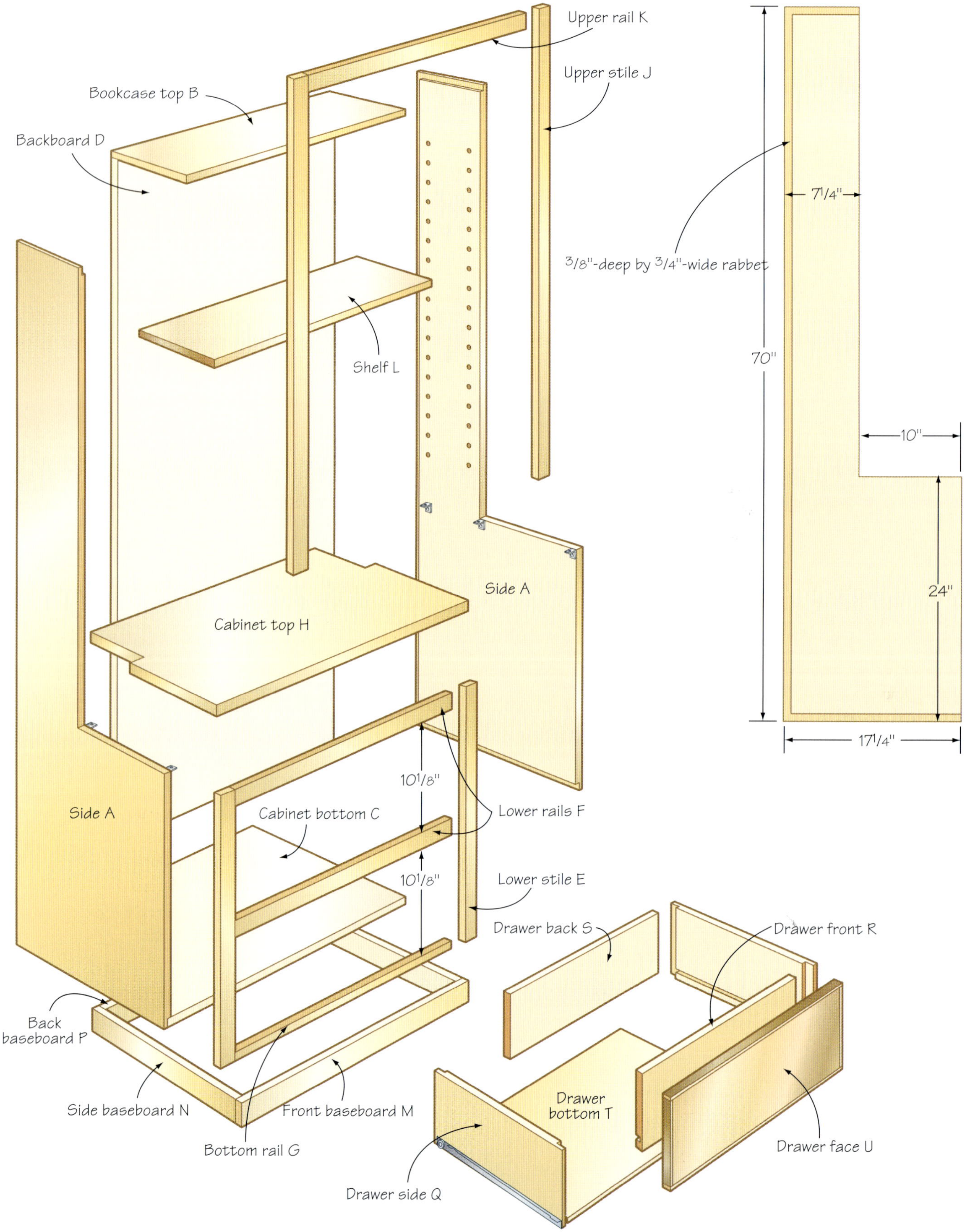
Upper rail K
Upper stile J
Bookcase top B
Backboard D
Shelf L
Side A
Cabinet top H
Side A
Cabinet bottom C
Lower rails F
Lower stile E
10 1/8"
10 1/8"
Back baseboard P
Side baseboard N
Front baseboard M
Bottom rail G
Drawer back S
Drawer front R
Drawer bottom T
Drawer face U
Drawer side Q
3/8"-deep by 3/4"-wide rabbet
7 1/4"
70"
10"
24"
17 1/4"

INCHES (MILLIMETERS)

REFERENCE	QUANTITY	PART	STOCK	THICKNESS	(mm)	WIDTH	(mm)	LENGTH	(mm)	COMMENTS
A	2	sides	veneer PB	3/4	(19)	17 1/4	(438)	70	(1778)	
B	1	bookcase top	veneer PB	3/4	(19)	7 1/4	(184)	23 1/4	(591)	
C	1	cabinet bottom	veneer PB	3/4	(19)	17 1/4	(438)	23 1/4	(591)	
D	1	backboard	veneer PB	3/4	(19)	23 1/4	(591)	68 1/2	(1740)	
E	2	lower stiles	solid wood	3/4	(19)	1 1/2	(38)	24	(610)	
F	2	lower rails	solid wood	3/4	(19)	1 1/2	(38)	21	(533)	
G	1	bottom rail	solid wood	3/4	(19)	3/4	(19)	21	(533)	
H	1	cabinet top	solid wood	1	(25)	18 1/4	(464)	26	(660)	
J	2	upper stiles	solid wood	3/4	(19)	1 1/2	(38)	45	(1143)	
K	1	upper rail	solid wood	3/4	(19)	1 1/2	(38)	21	(533)	
L	3	shelves	veneer PB	3/4	(19)	6 3/8	(162)	22 3/8	(568)	dimensions shown include a 1/2"-thick by 3/4"-high by 22 3/8" (13mm x 19mm x 568mm) solid wood edge glued and nailed with brads to the front edge of each shelf
M	1	front baseboard	solid wood	3/4	(19)	3 1/2	(89)	21	(533)	
N	2	side baseboards	solid wood	3/4	(19)	3 1/2	(89)	14 1/4	(362)	
P	1	back baseboard	solid wood	3/4	(19)	3 1/2	(89)	19 1/2	(495)	
Q	4	drawer sides	birch plywood	1/2	(13)	9 1/8	(232)	16	(406)	
R	2	drawer fronts	birch plywood	1/2	(13)	9 1/8	(232)	19 1/2	(495)	
S	2	drawer backs	birch plywood	1/2	(13)	8 3/8	(213)	19 1/2	(495)	
T	2	drawer bottoms	birch plywood	1/2	(13)	15 3/4	(400)	19 1/2	(495)	
U	2	drawer faces	veneer PB	3/4	(19)	11 1/8	(283)	22	(559)	drawer faces are 3/4" (19mm) PB banded with 3/4" x 1/2" (19mm x 13mm) solid wood

HARDWARE & SUPPLIES

right-angle metal brackets
glue
5/8" (16mm) screws
spiral finishing nails
2" (51mm) PB screws
2–16" (406mm) drawer glide sets
handles

SHOP TIP

Use the table saw to cut the reduced-width upper vertical section of the sides A to get a straight cut. Slowly approach the end of the cut, stopping 2" from the crosscut, and turn off the saw. Remove the side and repeat the procedures for the horizontal or crosscut. Score the outside of the uncut portion with a knife and complete the cut with a handsaw.

1 Cut the sides A as illustrated. The sides will require a rabbet that's 3⁄8" deep by 3⁄4" wide on the top, back and bottom edges. Attach the top B, back D and bottom C to the side panels A with glue and spiral finishing nails. Drive the nails from the back of each board into the edges of the sides A. Follow the same procedures as detailed for the dresser and assembly in this chapter. Make a shelf hole jig using any handy sheet material drilled with 2" spaced guide holes. Clamp it accurately in place and drill the holes.

2 Install three right-angle metal brackets per side. These will be used to secure the cabinet top H.

3 Install the lower stiles E and three rails F and G. Use glue and finishing nails following the same procedures as the dresser project for face frame installation. Then, round over the outside edge of the stiles and bottom rail with a 3⁄8" roundover bit.

4 Construct a base frame using parts M, N and P as detailed in the materials list. Once again, refer to the previous projects in this chapter for more details about building and installing the base fame.

5 Glue up the cabinet top H using 1"-thick material as detailed in chapter one "Making Solid Wood Panel Glue-Ups." Cut out a notch on both sides of the top H so it will fit tight against both cabinet sides A and the backboard D. Then, round over the top and bottom edge of the front and sides with a $\frac{3}{8}$" roundover bit. Do not round over the notched area or the back edge. Fit the top into the cabinet and secure it with screws in the right-angle brackets.

6 Attach the upper stiles J and rail K. Then round over the inner and outer edges of the frame with a $\frac{3}{8}$" router bit. Cut the shelves L to size as indicated in the materials list. Apply a wood strip to the front edge and test fit. Cut the drawer parts Q, R, S and T to the sizes shown in the materials list. Build the drawers following the instructions detailed in this chapter titled "Building Traditional Birch Plywood Drawers for Bottom-Mount Glides." Install the drawers, with 16" bottom-mount drawer glides, in the cabinet and attach the drawer faces U.

suppliers

Many suppliers have contributed products, material and technical support during the project building phase.

I appreciate how helpful they've been and recommend the companies without hesitation.

If you have trouble locating a product that I've mentioned, please e-mail me at danny@cabinetmaking.com.

Adams & Kennedy — The Wood Source
6178 Mitch Owen Road
P.O. Box 700
Manotick, Ontario
Canada K4M 1A6
613-822-6800
www.wood-source.com
Wood supply

Adjustable Clamp Company
417 North Ashland Avenue
Chicago, Illinois 60622
312-666-0640
www.adjustableclamp.com
Clamps

Blum Inc.
7733 Old Plank Road
Stanley, North Carolina 28164
704-827-1345
www.blum.com
Hinges, pocket-door hardware

Delta Machinery
4825 Highway 45 North
P.O. Box 2468
Jackson, Tennessee 38302-2468
800-223-7278 (U.S.)
800-463-3582 (Canada)
www.deltawoodworking.com
Woodworking tools

Exaktor Precision Woodworking Tools
136 Watline #182
Mississaugua, Ontario
Canada L4C 2E2
800-387-9789
www.exaktortools.com
Sliding table and other accessories for the table saw

General and General International
8360, du Champ-d'Eau
Montreal, Quebec
Canada H1P 1Y3
514-326-1161
www.general.ca
Woodworking tools

House of Tools Ltd.
100 Mayfield Common Northwest
Edmonton, Alberta
Canada T5P 4B3
800-661-3987
www.houseoftools.com
Woodworking tools and hardware

JessEm Tool Company
124 Big Bay Point Road
Barrie, Ontario
Canada L4N 9B4
866-272-7492
www.jessem.com
Rout-R-Slide and Rout-R-Lift

Knape & Vogt Manufacturing Company
2700 Oak Industrial Drive Northeast
Grand Rapids, Michigan 49505
616-459-3311
www.knapeandvogt.com
Drawer glides

Langevin & Forest
9995 Pie IX Boulevard
Montreal, Quebec
Canada H1Z 3X1
800-889-2060
www.langevinforest.com
Tools, hardware, lumber

Lee Valley Tools Ltd.
P.O. Box 1780
Ogdensburg, New York 13669-6780
800-871-8158 (U.S.)
800-267-8767 (Canada)
www.leevalley.com
Fine woodworking tools and hardware

Porter-Cable
4825 Highway 45 North
P.O. Box 2468
Jackson, Tennessee 38302-2468
888-848-5175
www.porter-cable.com
Woodworking tools

Richelieu Hardware
7900, West Henri-Bourassa
Ville St-Laurent, Quebec
Canada H4S 1V4
800-619-5446 (U.S.)
800-361-6000 (Canada)
www.richelieu.com
Hardware supplies to the professional trade

Rockler Woodworking and Hardware
4365 Willow Drive
Medina, Minnesota 55340
800-279-4441
www.rockler.com
Woodworking tools and hardware

Trend Machinery & Cutting Tools Ltd.
Odhams Trading Estate
St. Albans Road
Watford
Hertfordshire, U.K.
WD24 7TR
01923 224657
www.trendmachinery.co.uk
Woodworking tools and hardware

Vaughan & Bushnell Mfg. Co.
11414 Maple Avenue
Hebron, Illinois 60034
815-648-2446
www.vaughanmfg.com
Hammers and other tools

Wolfcraft North America
333 Swift Road
Addison, Illinois 60601-1448
630-773-4777
www.wolfcraft.com
Woodworking hardware

Woodcraft
P.O. Box 1686
Parkersburg, West Virginia 26102-1686
800-535-4482
www.woodcraft.com
Woodworking hardware

Woodworker's Hardware
P.O. Box 180
Sauk Rapids, Minnesota 56379-0180
800-383-0130
www.wwhardware.com
Woodworking hardware

Plywood and Particleboard material information and suppliers can be found at the Panolam or Uniboard sites
www.panolam.com
www.uniboard.com

index

More Great Projects from Danny Proulx and Popular Woodworking Books!

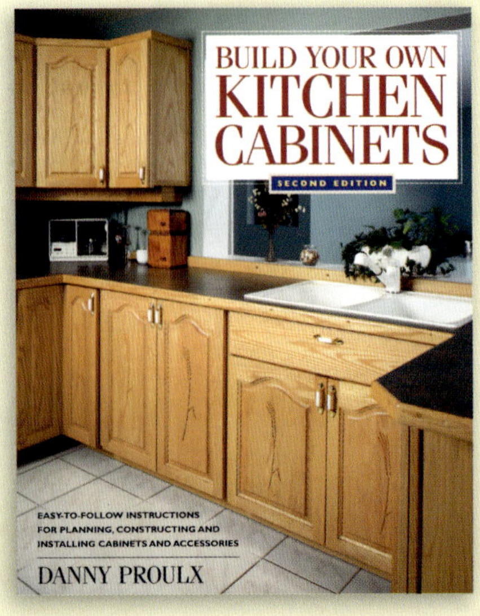

Save thousands of dollars by building your own custom kitchen cabinets – it's easier than you think with Danny Proulx's ingenious construction system. It's fast and doesn't require a lot of tools. Proulx's system combines the best parts of the face-frame cabinet-construction system that's common in North America and the European frameless cabinet system developed after World War II. The result is a cabinet that's easy to build, easy to install, easy to clean and looks like a traditional wooden cabinet.

ISBN 1-55870-676-3, paperback, 128 pages, #70626-K

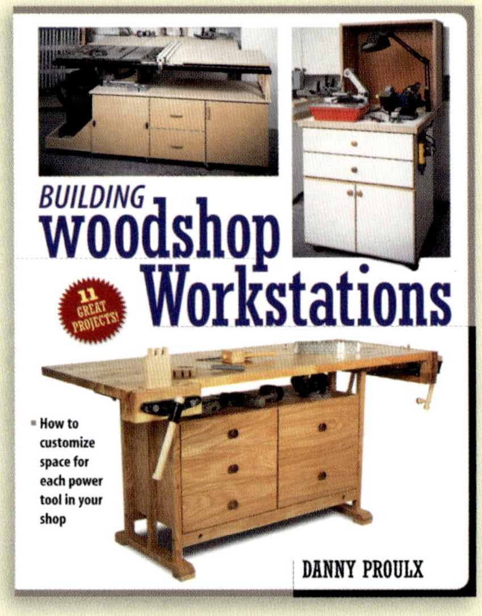

The 13 projects in *Building Woodshop Workstations* are carefully designed to do double duty in your shop: Not only will they store every tool, jig and accessory you own, many of them also will make your existing tools more accurate and easier to use. And best of all, this book shows you how to build these cabinets using quick, sturdy and material-efficient methods.

ISBN 1-55870-637-2, paperback, 128 pages, #70585-K

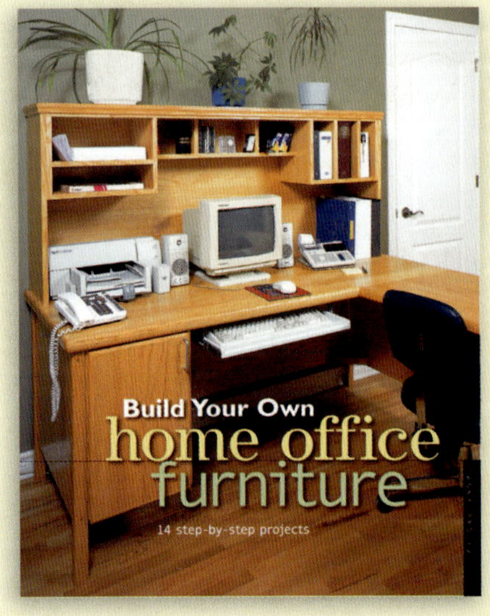

Transform any room into the perfect workspace! Inside you'll find invaluable tips and advice, plus 15 fresh, functional, fun-to-build projects packed with detailed photographs and step-by-step instructions. Designs range from simple storage modules to a computer desk/workstation, so no matter what your skill level, you'll find plenty of woodshop excitement.

ISBN 1-55870-561-9, paperback, 128 pages, #70489-K

When professional cabinetmaker Danny Proulx bought a pocket hole jig for his business he found ways to make it work even faster and harder—and he wrote a book about it so you can find out, too. *The Pocket Hole Drilling Project Book* is filled with 11 project plans built almost entirely using pocket hole jigs—plus advice and wisdom that comes from using these jigs to bore hundreds and hundreds of holes.

ISBN 1-55870-687-9, paperback, 128 pages, #70637-K

These and other great woodworking books are available at your local bookstore, woodworking stores, online suppliers or by calling 1-800-448-0915. When calling please use savings code TBA05PWB.